Bob Bickford is a goddamn revelation. His writing is so amazing, so vivid and sensory that it feels like a memory rising from the deepest part of yourself. A truth you have always carried in your bones. That's how it feels. And Christ, it is beautiful.

Michael Murray, *Galaxy Brain Magazine*

…a writer of immense talent, brings beautiful form from the mists of his subconscious.

Rebeccas Blissett, author of *Fused*

Dear Ghost

Bob Bickford

Paranormalice Press, LLC
www.paranormalice.com
paranormalicepress@gmail.com
Cover Art by Chris Holmes
Photos credit to Donnez Cardoza
Produced in the U.S.A

For you.

Sometimes I wonder, (when I fall asleep):

If all our days are really pressed into albums, dried flowers and crayons and photographs of people we barely remember, will we sit together later, flipping pages and pointing? You'll glance at me, say "look!" and show me the pattern of numbers and colors.

Then all at once, everything will make sense. We'll laugh and say of-course-why-didn't-we-see-it?

(Our ghosts were never white.)

Dear Ghost,

You told me once that everything perfect begins with an ending. I didn't know quite what you meant then, but now I'm trying to find out.

Since I don't know what else to do, I follow the dog.

He always knows when you're nearby. Since he was a baby, he's gotten to his feet and waited at the door with your car still two blocks away. You told me once that whenever you opened your eyes from a particularly vivid dream, he'd be awake in the dark. His eyes would shine from the foot of the bed, and you'd whisper to him. You'd ask if he'd dreamed your dream, too.

I wonder if you're dreaming now, one of your vivid dreams. I wonder if you dream you're gone. I'm dreaming a terrible dream too, about you-not-here.

The dog will know when you've come back, and that comforts me. I tell myself that he'll sense you and let me know. The dog can see you, even when you're vapor. When you're close, he'll tell me.

When I was eleven, a guy named Turk Broda died. I saw it on the news.

He wasn't the first dead guy I knew about. I understood in a vague way that people got old and died. I knew something about getting old and dying, because when I was little I spent some time in a nursing home.

After we left California but before we moved to Canada, we lived for a little while in Kansas. I delivered newspapers. A canvas bag printed 'HALSTEAD

GAZETTE' draped over the handlebars of my Stingray, papers rolled tight and rubber-banded. Lean the bike, fling-and-spin, thump against a screen door, and I was pretty damn glorious for a little kid. (I couldn't do it now, even if I'd secretly like to try.) Once in a while, I had to put the kickstand down and get one out of somebody's honeysuckle bush, blushing because some imaginary little girl might be watching from a window—but hey, Maury Wills parked the occasional double play toss in the front row seats, too.

The only other time I got off my bike was at the nursing home. Nobody called them 'retirement villas' in those distant days. I had about a dozen customers inside, and I had to walk the halls looking at room numbers. Nobody explained to me about dementia or the effects of strokes. They just sent me in, by myself. The oldstimers who followed me around, shouted at me, and asked garbled questions, didn't want to kill me. They were probably perfectly nice people, but as a group they terrified me to a degree I can't describe.

(These days my closest, most beloved friends are all over eighty, and I can see the clubhouse turn myself—but the memory still scares me a little.)

A little old guy with a white crew-cut took to playing hide-and-seek with me in the halls, popping from doorways and skittering away. That made too much. I couldn't make myself do it anymore. The nursing home complained to the newspaper. In due time, my parents got a report that every day I dumped a pile of papers on the reception desk and ran for my life. Mercifully, that was the end of that. The grownups in charge took the place off my route.

Anyway, I digress. Turk Broda shocked me deeply. He had been a goaltender for the Toronto Maple Leafs. I loved hockey. I loved goalies and felt determined to be one. They were modern knights, in their padded armor and anonymous facemasks. Turk had won five championships. My dad told me he just got old.

He was a hero, and (until then) heroes didn't get old and die. It didn't make sense. I brooded about his death because that's how I did things.

I had to write a story for a school assignment. I hated school, but I loved stories. This one still makes me blush, but I'll tell it anyway. Blushing is important—because that's when things are real and true.

I wrote about the deciding game of a hockey championship. The Toronto Maple Leafs were hopelessly outmatched, badly outplayed, and a loss looked likely. When their goalie got injured and carried off on a stretcher, any hopes for a miracle were gone. Surprise! A replacement goaltender skated out to take his place. The crowd buzzed, because he wore a number nobody recognized, and of course he remained incognito behind his facemask. The game resumed, and naturally the mystery man was terrific—because he was a hero, and that's what heroes do. They save the day. When the final horn sounded, the Leafs were champions. Behind the celebration at center ice, the unknown goalie quietly skated off and disappeared.

Afterward, when the players got back to the dressing room, they found a neat pile of equipment, with a mask on top. A note had been pinned to the pile, which read, "Best wishes—Turk." When everyone needed him most, the ghost came back—because that's what ghosts do, when they're heroes. They come back to the people who miss them.

So that's how I dealt with Turk. I wrote a letter.

I got a really good mark—not usual for me. That night, my mom checked my homework, as always. She was petite and pretty, and—severe. Tough. I think when she saw the grade, she probably wondered if the teacher had gone soft, so she sat at the kitchen table to read it, with me in attendance. She started out a little grim. When she finished, I realized she was crying.

Crying. My mom. Over a story I wrote. What the hell.

When you're eleven everything is still possible, even if it won't be for much longer. You race your bike for the checkered flag in the Indy 500. You play street hockey in front of your house for the Stanley Cup. You fall asleep sure that someday you'll rescue the girl who sits in the front row of class (and doesn't know you exist) from a burning building surrounded by monsters. Naturally, she loves you forever.

By the time you're twelve, you start deciding stories are bullshit. The real world mostly encourages that decision. The real world rewards the end of magic, the accumulation of common sense and dark opinions and clever victories and money. The real world isn't about stories.

All the same, the sheer wonder—the power—of my mom crying at the kitchen table eclipsed everything in my experience. I still feel it. I don't think about it too often, so it doesn't get diluted. I still chase that moment, every day of my life. If your eleven-year-old self likes you, you've got a shot at happily-ever-after. That's it, and that's all. So there.

I write you letters, ghost, and I keep an eye on the dog. When he goes to the door and sits, I'll know I wrote a spell and brought you back.

Dear Ghost,

Black pepper tastes like every color mixed together, and that reminds me of 1985. I wish I could write faster. I wish I could think faster.

I love the sad, cloying time that downtowns in small cities always get on Friday evening. I lived for a while in the middle of Santa Barbara, and I walked home in the curious, lingering hour between day and night, the warm half-light you only see in southern California. The shoppers and the office people had left, and the tourists were back in their hotels. The dying sun threw shadows in a city staged just for me. I sensed the crazies, like feral children, waiting for full dark to come out.

If I go back there now, I'll remember I'm lonely.

Come with me to 1985, and I'll point at the street, at a late delivery beer truck that says 'Pabst Blue Ribbon' squeezing between brick walls lining an alley. Chaka Khan echoes, "I Feel for You" from a car radio. We'll see office windows gone dark for the weekend, and the bars and restaurants beneath them lighting up and getting ready. A guy moves tables onto a sidewalk patio, while a woman smokes a cigarette and watches him.

Twilight turns the clouds green, and you'll contemplate neon signs already turned on for the night, pink and blue glow. We'll see the rising moon and the sky, smell the ocean five blocks down. We'll walk the gathering dark then, and I'll point out balconies just because they look nice.

You'll ask me if I'm homesick, and

I'll whisper all the secrets you've never heard before and tell you all the things you're going to know later. You'll remind me that the past, and the now, and the what's-coming, make a pattern that's rushing together. Good always moves to the center, and the lost and hurt parts will make sense, someday. Even the heart-stab regrets eventually fit, breathe easy, turn sweet.

You'll lead me past a swimming pool that moves, through trees, real dirt and warm stones, green life everywhere in the dark, all the colors of pepper, and then into long rooms filled with golden light.

1985 will come true, if we wait long enough.

Dear Ghost,

Near the downtown part of a city that I don't much like, a small restaurant stood at the edge of a park. When I was young, I walked past it on my way to work every morning. It had colored lights and a courtyard and live music on the weekends, and I heard the waiters were all beautiful and only spoke French. People sat outside at night, behind fancy railings, drinking Grand Marnier or champagne cocktails and looking at trees in the dark.

I never had the money to go there when I was starting out and it was open. The young woman I thought I loved asked for it frequently, and I promised, but we never did.

She went there on her very first date with someone else.

I still walked past the restaurant every morning. I could have gone to work a different way, but maybe the hurt, imagining her walking the same sidewalk, drinking a white wine spritzer and laughing at someone else's silly jokes, made a way to keep the last trace of her with me.

A path ran away from the restaurant into the park, past trees and benches and then around a bend and out of sight. It felt like a path that went somewhere, even though I knew it only led to swing sets and a community center and a football field. Weeping willows bent over either side, and I often had the absurd thought, hurrying by in the mornings after the young woman left, that Ratty and Mole and Badger were nearby.

I resisted the urge to abandon everything and turn onto the path. (In those days, I thought it good and grownup to avoid childish places.) I thought about first dates instead. My heart hurt every time like the first time, and magic didn't matter.

Now the restaurant is gone, and I don't live in that city anymore. The park is still there, though. I checked Google maps.

Last night you told me, ghost, that the restaurant had been a doorway to the Askew, back when I was young. It's still there, still on the Askew map, and the pretty people are still ordering drinks in French. Just past the willow-tree bend, the path I never took joins a miniature river that falls down rocks and waterfall into a pond. Dark shade, long grass, bright-colored birds, and if I listen carefully there's music behind the waterfall noise.

You said once I pass the bend, the fragrance is green, wet, and slightly salty. You said the more alive things are, the better they smell. That's why puppies smell so good, and why the ocean smells better than perfume. You added that of course Ratty and Mole are real, as if anyone could make them up.

You told me it's all so beautiful I might faint.

I told you I've never fainted, and also that I don't think I've ever danced with anyone in the kind of way that matters, because I never danced with you.

You nodded, and I could tell that made you happy.

You said that every day I walked past the restaurant-on-the-park, you had been there, sitting on the grass just around the willow-bend and making a crown of flowers for the dog sitting beside you. You watched the younger me walk by, and you waved.

I didn't know you were there then, but now I do.

Dear Ghost,

At three o'clock, the phantoms come out. They are antique but oh so young, and they look at each other, eyes wet, and marvel at their own colors.

Toronto city, between summer night and summer morning, and this might be Dupont or Summerhill, with a plumber's van parked at the curb. Across the street, a church and a lit billboard and the air outside feels cool after the day-heat still trapped upstairs. Behind me, the door lock snicks and it's final. I can't go back inside, so maybe I'll walk up to Eglinton Avenue, and all the sidewalks are empty but they echo with Blondie and white light and spit and orange soda.

Look down to light a cigarette, and I remember the Adidas on my feet—I'll lose them later on a beach in California in a different darkness, walk home drunk and barefoot—and that loss worries me, even though I don't know about it yet.

1982 is just a thin skin over tonight, and thousands of miles away and almost forty years in the future a girl-turned-woman looks from a window and remembers where she was right now, and if I remembered her better, I'd start walking west and get there when I'm old.

I'm so tired my eyes hurt, but sleep hurts worse and there's nowhere to sleep, anyway. Tonight, the street will take me somewhere if I can find it before daylight traps. Miles to the south, the rides at the lakefront are still spinning colored light and popcorn noise and last year I went there, but now those days are gone and I'm glad I don't know I'll never be there again. Some things happen only once.

A bandshell concert, baseball and…

A diner on Davenport Road is dark from the outside, but inside the space is gold and heavy with vinegar mixed with egg-and-cigarettes. They smoke Export 'A' Green in this part of town. The place is full, as if the people have all left the street to squeeze inside. The voices are loud and confident, like they have a place to be at this time of night and it's here, with the bacon and glass ashtrays and little jukeboxes that don't work—but it's a lie. They can't go outside. If they try, they'll deflate and tumble into nothing, so they'll stay here forever.

The laughter rises because these people are as scared as I am, of the outside and time—phantom daytime crowds prowling the sidewalks, insisting life goes on—and I'm not that, but I'm not this either, so they watch me.

I ask for coffee, and the woman behind the counter squints and gets a little impatient with my change because she knows I'm not even real. I can't stay here, with these people, her people, who are long gone. She squeezes the Styrofoam cup into a small paper bag and folds the top closed before she gives it to me. It isn't coffee for drinking: it's a cream-and-sugar charm to take with me, a flashlight.

I carry it outside and smell the city at night.

The cup-in-bag will still be warm in a hundred years, and I'll still be walking here. A letter's been riding in my pocket, for a time. St. Clair Avenue is two blocks north and there's bound to be a mailbox.

That has to be enough, for now.

Dear Ghost,

I dreamed I had breakfast with my mom. I knew I was dreaming, the whole time.

Afterward, we stood together on the sidewalk outside the restaurant. It seemed like a funny kind of dream since I never eat breakfast—and as far as I can remember, neither did she. Maybe we just recited the menus out loud, trying to find secret messages, and then dropped a tip on the table and left. I told her so, and it made her laugh.

"Is that what this is?" she asked me. "A dream?"

"It's the middle of the night. We wouldn't be having breakfast now, unless this was a dream."

I had forgotten the sound of her, and it made me feel good. I had also forgotten how pretty she was, or maybe I never noticed. Behind her, neon glowed green with restaurant business, and a cement planter burst with red blossoms. The city stirred, warm gusts of breeze and streams of tinted lights, over and around us.

"I think I've been here before—haven't I?"

She laughed again. "If you say so. It's your dream."

Once when I was a teenager, I got off a Greyhound bus in a distant western city I had never been to before. A little distance from the station, I stood on a curb waiting for a light to turn green, and suddenly felt sure I had stood at that intersection before. I remembered the street signs and palm trees I had never seen before. I traced the tops of the hills above the city with my eyes, speaking their names under my breath. I knew all of it.

I felt completely certain that my house sat two blocks up, one block over. I had been away—and come home.

Nineteen years old and sure of things, I shook the feeling off. I shrugged my backpack higher, crossed at the green, went the opposite direction, and got on with my life. I've spent the rest of my years walking away and not remembering the moment.

Now I was back.

I looked at the time. I haven't worn a wristwatch in decades, but this one felt black-and-white familiar, and mine from another life. I buckled the worn leather strap on every morning because you gave the watch to me, ghost, once upon a time. You got the back engraved with whatever name you wore in that different life, and you told me it would keep you close. I felt the letters of you against my skin.

"I'm late," I told my mom. "I gotta run."

I gestured at the suitcase full of dirty clothes waiting on the sidewalk at my feet. I had a job, planes and trains, places to be, calls to make. I had a million things I had to do, even if I couldn't recall one of them. I got flooded with sad.

"It's okay," she said. "You're not wrong. I'll see you around."

She looked back over her shoulder at me, just once, walking away. I realized she was at least twenty years younger than me, and that made me smile. Dreams are funny. She smiled back, like she read my mind. I felt happy, warm, watching her. I hope I see her again.

I called my job to say I was late. They didn't care. I picked up the suitcase.

Everything is alive, ghost. You told me once that everything perfect begins with an ending, and nothing perfect ever ends. I think I'm starting to understand—warm winds and soft lights, the fragrances of flowers and faraway places, the letters and numbers in your name.

Two blocks up, one over. Next time. I won't forget.

Dear Ghost,

Remember when you told me about parallel parking? You never really had to learn, not the awkward teenager way the rest of us did. You saw a diagram, drawn with chalk. It made perfect sense, so you went outside and echoed it perfectly in a car. Just like so, and just like that.

Everything is simple, about echoes, you say. It's just knowing how to tilt your head and squint. Ghosts only move in the corners of eyes, and you're a ghost so you should know.

It's 5:15 in the morning. Early summer here, and it's supposed to be dark, but I can see. That's the thing I like best about summer—it's usually light outside. Things glow, even in the dark. Rachael Yamagata sings "Over and Over" from my tiny speakers, looping over and over. You're probably asleep, because ghosts dream too, and there's a dragon egg beside your bed, lit blue.

I think a lot about forever, lately.

There's a house on the corner of 20th and Pine, in Halstead, Kansas. It was our house, once—mom and dad and seven kids, and our granddad, too. Our back-then neighbor told me the house has been occupied for many years now by a lonely man, all by himself, who is quite proud of it. The grass my dad used to burn when it got too long for his machete looks like a green golf course. There's a new front door, and the upended tricycles and my mom's dead 1956 Plymouth Belvedere are gone from the driveway.

The scraggly pine tree I used to climb in the front yard (I dreamed about the top but was never brave enough) has been cut down and replaced with something decorative— a Japanese maple, maybe. Something beautiful, with purple leaves that never tolerated children.

Sometimes I wonder if phantoms wander the place, laughing and crying. Our memories, the echoes of us little, more vivid than we were in life.

After dinner, my grandfather stood at the curb in front of the house, watching the road. In my recollection, he always wears a metal eye patch, from cataract surgery. He smokes the one Lucky Strike my mom allows him each evening, since she heard the Surgeon General's report. I think it was his favorite time, and he went out to be by himself. He's still there I think, holding his cigarette between finger and thumb, barely visible in the twilight. Ghosts go back to their favorite things.

(Remember that when you're sad.)

I wonder if the new owner ever hears splashing in the garage that he built on the spot where we had our pool. My sister had a transistor radio, and I swam in cold water from the hose the first time I heard Frankie Valli sing "You're Just Too Good to be True". I fell in love with someone I couldn't see—and started looking west, without being aware. It would be decades before I knew that wasn't really the name of the song. It's still too good to be true, and I'm not lost anymore.

(Even if you're a ghost, don't die first. When we're both gone, meet me at the green house on Pine Street.)

Perhaps the man, the new owner, keeps the door to the smallest upstairs bedroom closed, the spare one my mom designated a "playroom". We rarely played in it, because it had a very bad shadow that hadn't been dead long and was still angry. Opening the toy box always ended up with hitting and pinching and pulling hair. I'm sitting here, years and years later, and wondering how a family with seven kids and a grandfather possibly kept a spare bedroom. It dawns on me that my mom must have seen the shadow too, so nobody slept there.

Maybe a dog named Smokey still wanders the back yard. He's buried near the new garage, but I'm sure the man doesn't know about his bones. Smokey was big and yellow. He belonged to friends in California, before we packed and moved to small town Kansas. My parents visited them a lot, and he fell in love with my dad. One day he showed up at our door, looking for him. It was a story that got repeated, because in family lore we lived a hundred miles away. I know that isn't true, but it made a long way on desert highways, regardless. My dad put him in the car and took him back, but a week later he showed up again. Everyone agreed he had found his true home, and it was for the best he came and lived with us. So, he did.

An old boy, he barely tolerated children. He didn't want to play, and might snap if you tried, so he just hovered at the edges, always moving through the childhood scenery. He still lingers, in the pink and green and gold long ago.

Dogs were put out in the morning and came home at night. Sometimes, if you were walking to the library, you'd see your dog crossing the street and say hello and keep going. Smokey got hit by a car and the impact broke his back legs. He wore casts with blood seeping from them. When the plaster came off, he was too slow to get out of the way anymore so it happened again, and maybe even a third time. By some miracle, he survived all the cars and died of old age. One afternoon he stood out in the yard, and he threw up and fell over.

My dad wanted to be by himself when he buried him.

When we leave, the people who remember us, who remember our laugh and our favorite ice cream, gradually vanish. They disappear too, one by one. It comforts me that this business is now between my dad and Smokey, so it doesn't matter if their story leaves with me (and now you). It gives me the idea that love doesn't depend on knowing where the bones are.

No matter how much I write, I can't tell you everything because some stories don't have words. I use crayons and do my best. Sitting here with the dark-light summer morning outside, I can only tell you that there's no sadness in faded Polaroids. It all unfolds the way it's supposed to.

I know these things because you told me about parallel parking. I've never stopped looking, and I found the song that still plays on the radio by a small swimming pool in 1967, didn't I? Someday I'll get to the top of the scraggly pine tree I never climbed.

The oldest pictures of when we were little haven't even been taken yet. The Polaroids always move, never end, never stop, never die.

I'll see you on Pine Street.

Dear Ghost,

Someday, I want you to wake me up in the middle of the night because it's raining. I'll say that I want to go for a walk, and you'll be happy because that's what you were thinking, too.

(Dear Ghost, When we were little)

I got left behind in a Mississippi gas station once, at midnight.

Driving all night, asleep in the back of a rental Buick Wildcat, and we coasted in under the lights and the engine shut down. The quiet ticked, and my parents spoke in low voices. I always loved it when they talked to each other too low to be overheard. Not whispers, just the shorthand murmuration of people who know each other's warmth and smell in the middle of the night. It told me they had lives other than what I saw, that they were real people who had business with each other besides me. It made me safe.

They got out of the car, quietly, a snicking of latches on either side, and their voices moved off. I had time, I thought. After a moment, I got out too, and breathed in the different world.

Mississippi smells different than anywhere else, at midnight. The black air is so warm it washes against your skin like underwater. In the distance, dogs bark. On the highway, semi-trucks are snoring dragons as they slow down. Electric lights don't do much against Mississippi darkness. It all feels slow and sweet and dangerous.

The Gulf sign glowed orange and buzzed. A halo of moths swarmed around it, frantic to reach the unreachable light. In the shadows beside the station, the corpse of an automobile rested, its front end smashed into something unrecognizable. I wandered over for a look. The back remained a Chevy Biscayne, pretty new. I had enough light to see the dealer sticker on the trunk. Hattiesburg, it said. I didn't know where Hattiesburg was, but the car was never going back there.

A little further in, I saw a humped line of more derelicts. I loved cars, and I loved old cars that had lost their drivers most. I wandered deeper. Too dark to investigate, and the dead cars seemed to sense me there. I already knew what ghosts felt like, even then, and there came a stirring I recognized. I skedaddled. If you don't pump your arms, it looks like fast walking and not running in case anyone is looking. I rounded the corner, back into light, and...

The Buick was gone.

The cement in front of the pumps sat as empty as if my parents had always been my imagination. The Gulf sign buzzed bright, and the moths swarmed. I thought if I stayed perfectly still, the impossibility I looked at might change, but it didn't. I was alone.

I didn't know what to do. I headed for the fluorescents in the gas station office because it was the only thing I could think of.

Filling stations didn't have 7-Elevens in those days. They weren't the places I go at midnight to get a hot dog and a Coke slush when I can't sleep. Those days would come later. Back then, they were daytime about hot sun and gasoline and tire changes and dirty hands and tow trucks. Change got made out of a drawer in an office that reeked of motor oil and cigarette smoke.

At night, gas stations were about bad business. Especially gas stations at midnight, outside Hattiesburg, Mississippi. Four men sat in the office. They didn't ask me what I was doing, a small boy alone in the middle of the night. They looked through me and decided I must be invisible. They went back to saving their hideous world, back to their darkness, their beer and ball caps and hate. One of the men held an automatic pistol in his lap. I didn't need Freud or teenaged wisdom to understand his gun-caresses looked exactly like what they were.

I found a plastic chair and sat there for a while in the cigarette smell and fluorescent light. It's not hard to be tough when you're little. Nobody has come along yet to say different. You are what you are. I think I've always known about dragons and what they mean to me.

Back outside seemed like a better idea. The bell over the door tinkled as I went out.

I found some pebbles on the dark asphalt. I like touching sand and rocks when I'm in strange places. No matter how distant, dirt is where I came from—and it feels like home because it is. Our mother's skin, wherever we are, forever and always. I rolled the pebbles against my fingers, watched the dark road and waited.

Sure enough, the pebbles worked.

I'd like to believe they were charmed, because I still have some road to walk and I might need them again later. I also believe that my mom's radar stayed just about perfect, and it would have been blaring alarms in her head before the Buick got more than a couple miles south. Headlights approached like I had conjured them. It's funny how you always know the lights that are coming to rescue you.

I don't remember my mom and dad even being mad or saying much. Get in. I curled safe in the back seat, asleep almost before my dad wheeled us back on the highway. Sometimes I hope when I die, I see 1967 Buick Wildcat headlights getting bigger, and my mom rolls down the passenger window as it coasts up.

Get in.

I can't wait to make you laugh again, ghost. For now, the moments of you get caught by the wind, Polaroids blown like leaves. I run after them and I stuff my pockets, but some get lost. I still hold pebbles, and I still know which way is west. Someday, that same wind will scatter me into the Pacific. The currents know you and will float me home.

Promise you'll wake me in the middle of the night, whenever it rains.

Dear Ghost,

We're ghosts, ghost.

I write you letters as I'm falling asleep, and you read them somewhere else. We can't see each other, but you turn the dream-pages and hear my voice. I feel your smile. The night smells different when it's really dark air, a breath of forever coming through the open window. I turn my pillow to the cool side, and things get quiet.

The frogs stop singing, and that's when the train comes. You're on board, cheek pressed to glass, watching the night roll by. Watching for me.

It's funny how the sound of a train at night means— everything. The horn is a saxophone, faint wheels-on-rails make a left-handed piano counterpoint, gates come down and red-light bells play the drums. I close my eyes tight and watch the rows of lighted windows stream past the crossing, trying to see you.

People inside sway slightly as they walk up the aisles, touching seat backs in time to the beat of steel wheels. Some read magazines and slap cards, others have a last whiskey-and-soda in the club car. My bed turns into a cold berth, and I'm there. Lights from passing towns make patterns on the ceiling, and it's all strange but the train rocks and rocks, says shhhh-sleep-you're-safe-shhhh-sleep-you're-safe.

I get up anyway, and prowl. The next car is dim. I spot a little kid with a crew cut kneeling on his seat, wide-eyed and way past his bedtime, watching the world go by. I remember myself, but he doesn't recognize me. He has no suspicion he'll grow up and get old. We both wear rumpled t-shirts and sandals, which makes me smile. I haven't changed that much. I sketch him a wave and keep going. I know where he's headed.

We went back to visit California in 1967, but you were gone. You moved away the year after we did. I was still little, and we took the train from Wichita, Kansas all the way to the Pacific Ocean.

San Diego had pearl divers, a river of bright Volkswagens, and supermarkets. Frank Sinatra Junior sang in the hotel lounge. There were jellyfish washed up on the sand, a new beach ball, and a dog who didn't seem to belong to anyone. I figured he ought to come home with us, but my mom said no. Furious, I told her I didn't see one goddamned good reason why not. And got smacked.

All that's a different story, but tonight I'm back on the train, starting out.

Our little Kansas town, Halstead, had a train station, but it hadn't been used for passengers since cowboy days, so we drove east, the wrong direction, to the Wichita train station in the middle of the night and left the car in the parking lot. My dad carried the suitcases to the platform and my mom worried about all the things we probably forgot to pack. We boarded the Super Chief, and the conductor acted like meeting a little kid at one o'clock in the morning was the nicest thing that ever happened to him. He had been working since Chicago, and he helped me with the metal steps and we were already friends.

I asked him why the train had a name. He told me why it was the Super Chief, but it's been a lot of years and I've forgotten his answer. I know now that we knew each other before that night, and I'll see him again someday. I'll ask him, then.

The train shuddered and pulled out, left the Wichita city lights behind. We backtracked through the night and a half hour later slowed and stopped in Halstead to take on the mail. I stared through the window at the dark town like I saw a magic trick. We were a couple of hours into the biggest adventure of my life, and right back where we started.

I shook my dad awake. "Look!"

He explained things to me and told me to go to sleep. I couldn't explain the Askew to him. I looked at the same streets I had been on that day, but the world had changed. I was different, now. Out there under the streetlights stood the library, my school, our house. My friends were all asleep behind darkened windows, completely unaware I sat here on the train, seeing them from a different place. The town didn't know I wasn't gone. In the morning, everyone would wake up and go on without me.

It felt exciting and magic, and it hurt my heart. I couldn't articulate homesickness for a place I hadn't left.

That's all forever is, ghost. It's all the train. The people who have left us sit behind lighted windows, waving. We're asleep in our dark town, listening for train horns. We just can't see each other.

So even if I can't see you, wave to me. We're always together, and we stay colored by our promises. The night is sweet, and the ones we love aren't ever gone. We all end up in San Diego, sooner or later.

Shhhh-sleep-you're-safe-shhhh-sleep-you're-safe-shhhh-sleep-you're-safe-shhhh...

Dear Ghost,

When we were little, I shared the back seat of a '56 Plymouth with a jumble of moving boxes. You stood across the street, on the sidewalk in front of your house, watching. Solemn face, honeyed skin, dark eyes, sweet premonitions. Brake-squeak at the end of Loma Linda Avenue, and then we puffed smoke and turned left onto North Serrano. I watched you through the back window, smaller and smaller, until you weren't there.

Our houses are apartment buildings now, which makes me feel funny. The big world, the people we saw hurrying along the sidewalks, with grocery bags and library books and dogs on leashes, are all gone. Loma Linda Avenue is still there. Hollywood and Sunset Boulevards, Western and Franklin and Los Feliz, run as busy as they ever did. Nobody remembers us. Nobody on their way to dinner and drinks has any idea we were ever there.

We're ghosts, ghost.

Through all the California days of my life, San Diego had pearl divers, Santa Barbara had Michael Jackson, San Francisco had candlesticks and chopsticks, Hollywood had ice cream, Morro Bay had dark hills and fish and gold sunsets.

Once, California had us—when we were little.

It will have us again because I'll see you there. One day, I'll be waiting for a light to turn green so I can cross a street, thinking about something else, and I'll glance over to see you standing beside me. The look on my face will make you laugh.

Ever traveling, and I'm tired but the current feels gentler now. It still flows west, but it's broadening. The sky looks different, and lovely.

Wait.

Dear Ghost,

I sat by myself in the left field bleachers at Royal Stadium, one September night when I was considerably younger than I am now. A hard wind had blown me into Kansas City—two weeks earlier I would never have imagined myself there. Life turns on a dime, and I had wandered into a strange Missouri city, homesick but without the slightest idea of what place I missed. There seemed to be no next place.

A baseball game, because I had nowhere better to be. The crowd was like me—they had nowhere else to go on a weeknight in early autumn. The pennant race unfolded miles away; the Royals finished thirteen games back that year. The shadow of Kirk Gibson batted .236 and they had no pitching. A good crowd though, a real baseball crowd, grateful to take in a nothing game. The sports pages point elsewhere when pennant hopes are gone, and baseball stops being television and goes back to being pure and timeless.

I've sat alone in airports, gas stations, and bus terminals in the middle of the night—but I've maybe never been lonelier than sitting alone in left field that night, holding onto a bag of popcorn. I wasn't going anywhere.

The bullpen beneath me, whistling pitches, snap of leather. Jim Eisenreich tossed a ball over the wall to a little kid a few rows in front of me, up late on a school night. People clapped because it made a nice thing for him to do—a baseball kind of thing.

Above me, clouds of moths swirled in the stadium lights. The dark felt warm, with just a tiny promise of cool underneath. In Missouri, they gaze at September skies, say winter is a hawk and they feel him coming when the wind blows. I had no jacket, but the night air still smelled of late summer.

I watched the moths, and things started to feel different and familiar. We've all been to the Midwest, because it's where we start. We all belong there, ghost, at least a little bit. We know the corn fields, the odor of rich dirt, the fragrance of our earth mother. We've sat on a porch, watching land so flat you see truck headlights on the highway two miles off and watch the red lights disappear for a full five minutes after the diesel snoring has gone by. We've sipped on a glass of warm Coca-Cola before heading up to bed.

We know train whistles at night, and we love the good perfume of sheets dried on the line. It's where we came from.

We also know baseball: hot dogs, clean white uniforms, green grass, the paint smell of bleachers in the sun—warm and eternal. Half the battle is knowing where you belong. Train stations in the middle of the night aren't so bad when you have a ticket home.

Something came clear, sitting by myself in Royal Stadium that night in mid-September, all those years ago. I was exactly where I belonged, and everything would turn out all right. I didn't need to know where I went next, only that I was going. I would move again, in my time. I had been holding my breath, and I let it out and watched baseball, happier than I'd been in a while.

I'm homesick for Hollywood in the summer of 1963. I miss the Santa Monica Pier, ice cream, Hershey bars, tail fins, and dark eyes. I miss your laugh. Someday, I'll cross the years and sift Pacific sand through my fingers. I won't have to leave, ever again—but part of me will always sit under the moth-lights in Kansas City, eating popcorn. I don't mind. I belong there, too.

We start going home the day we're born, ghost. I know that now. Everything is the road, everything is baseball, everything is forever, and everything is okay.

Dear Ghost,

I asked once what scared you, and you told me you were afraid of absolutely everything. I said you walked through the world anyway, with your chin up, so that made you the bravest person I knew.

So—Dear Ghost: here's a Letter, and a story.

When I was seven or eight, I met a kid. I don't know what dark business brought me into his orbit, but I see country road and a dirt parking lot, light poles with bugs flying through every halo. I hear a chorus of frogs singing loud in the night. I don't know why my parents pushed me in his direction and left for an hour. The circumstances don't matter, but the frogs do, because this is a story about frogs.

"You boys are the same age," my mom said when she introduced us, like it was some kind of happy miracle and she could never have imagined such a thing. "You'll have fun."

We were both white boys and the same age, so instant friendship got assumed. That's the source of most things wrong with the world, ghost—the insistence on seeing ourselves in the mirror of someone else. In my experience, tribes composed of like people are nothing but pure evil.

Left to our own devices, we both knew immediately we were nothing alike. He was one of those tanned, confident lords of the playground; tall for his age, blond hair worn a little long, madras shirt and boat shoes. Small for my age,

I wore black Keds with one broken lace and a crewcut. I loved Little League and wanted most of all, desperately, to be good at baseball, but I went to the batter's box a guaranteed strikeout. I always had buttons missing from my shirt and could never explain to my mom where they went.

I was scared of everything, too. Like you.

A lot of no-such-things followed me around in those days, and I imagine far to the west you were seeing them, too. I wish we wore Batman telephones on our wrists when I was eight and you were seven. As soon as mine flashed and beeped, I'd hold it to my ear and you'd be on the other end. We'd agree that of course there are "such-things", and that would be that. We'd decide whether we needed to do anything about them, or just keep walking scared with our chins up. We wouldn't have been alone.

I must have played with the kid more than once, even if I only remember the frog, because I knew a lot about him.

His parents were very young.

The father was a budding movie star who had gone to California to work on a film. He left behind a Corvette Stingray convertible, carelessly stored with one soft tire and the top down. I had never touched a Corvette before, and to this day the recollection feels holy. The car was a Hot Wheels come to life. Orange from a distance, up close the color changed. The metal-flake paint moved like water—flecks of gold and silver and copper mixed into hard candy.

The kid told me that his dad bought the car brand new and had it repainted metal-flake before he would even drive it, like that explained everything. Maybe it did— buying something that ordinary people dreamed of owning, but it wasn't good enough to drive off the showroom floor.

His mother was loud and pretty. She was trying to be in films too, and she filled the spaces around her with inappropriate laughter, beautiful hair, white teeth, and the perfume-stink of her fear. She moved around distracted, and every time her glance lit on her son, she shooed him with her fingers and told him to go play.

My parents whispered to each other, quiet so I wouldn't hear, that the movie star was never coming back. He had sent divorce papers from the west coast. I guess even beautiful hair and the Corvette couldn't keep him. A boy obviously hadn't made a difference. The starlet didn't know what would happen to her.

My dad said, quiet so she couldn't hear, that she never mentioned her son and some people had no business having a kid.

The boy got five dollars a week to spend, and more if he asked. Nobody kept track. His mom got a man-friend to drive him to any store he wanted. He bought new toys just to break them. It made a kind of fabulous, careless wealth that remains beyond my imagination, even today. Twenty-five cents in my pocket made a windfall that needed careful consideration before spending on a baseball or a balsa wood airplane. A dollar was too much to spend, and owning one meant I had to walk to the bank with my little passbook to add it to the six bucks or so I had saved for college.

(I didn't know what college actually was. As things happened, I never found out. Maybe I have six bucks in a small-town bank, still collecting interest.)

I remember night-time, and the frogs singing. The kid had something to show me. It wasn't a Corvette, and it wasn't a toy. Around the back of something, a place grownups couldn't see from a window or the parking lot, stood a wall. It had been spattered with gore. I didn't understand what I looked at until the kid told me it was dead frogs. I hadn't known blood turned black. He liked to throw them against the wall as hard as he could and watch them explode. He broke them, like he broke his toys.

From the darkness around us, the frogs sang.

I loved them. In those days, you could always catch a frog if you looked. My mom said never inside the house, and one hour was the maximum keeping-time. They had to be returned to someplace cool where they could see water if they wanted to. Sometimes, finding the right place and putting them back made the best part of the adventure.

Horror actually crawls. I can feel it still, fingers moving on my chest and neck, when I remember seeing that he held a frog. It was a big one, eyes shining from beneath his fingers. He told me to watch the wall, not the throw, or I would miss the moment.

I set my feet and told him to let the frog go.

"Make me," he said. "Maybe I'll kill you, instead."

Clearly the idea interested him, and I have no doubt he put it away for later.

"Make me," he said, again.

So, I did. I was small for my age and I couldn't hit a baseball out of the infield, but I had a big litter of brothers and sisters. We fought every day, sometimes for fun, and sometimes not—and we wore our bruises and missing clumps of hair with pride and never tattled. I knew fists and was practically a Kung-fu fighter, and this kid got everything he wanted and never had to fight anyone.

I slugged him, and he dropped the frog.

It was over pretty fast. I'd like to remember that I rode in on my skinny horse and rusty armor and beat the living hell out of him, but I think the truth has fewer colored flags. I imagine after I tossed a couple of wild punches, he lost interest. If he had to pay for something, he didn't want it.

The frog hadn't moved from where he dropped it. I cried while I found a cool place like my mom always said to. The frogs around me sang and sang, so there must have been water nearby.

The world changed that night, or maybe I did. I think the line between my sunlit childhood and the Askew dissolved—or maybe I just stopped believing there was a line. I know what evil is. If he's alive today, I have no doubt the kid has stayed busy all these years, breaking toys and frogs and people.

I wish I could tell you, ghost, that I saved all the frogs that have hopped into my path since. The truth is, I let most of them take their own chances. The world has its ways, and we're still afraid of it, you and I.

We walk though anyway, and the frogs still sing. I'm not scared when you're close by. I have a flashlight after all, and you have crumbs.

Dear Ghost,

I'm thinking about Time, and the way it bends when you're around.

In 1965 I rode east, across the country and away from you, in the back seat of a Plymouth. We stopped somewhere in the middle, muddy rivers and corn fields, for a few years. I have some dark memories of Kansas, because it's where I started to see ghosts, but that's not a story for now. Here's a pebble for your cigar box:

Summertime in the heartland, and we rode with Mrs. H, a friend of my mom's, in her blue Ford Galaxie. My mom drove really fast, so her friend always insisted on taking her own car when we went for a drive. Sunshine with clouds blowing across, dirt roads without names, barbed wire and tall crops. My mom leaning forward, a little impatient, because even if it was just a country drive, she wanted destinations. Her friend leaning back, dark glasses and cigarette, a couple of nail-polish fingers resting on the steering wheel.

Whenever I've read Erma Bombeck, I've thought of Mrs. H. She rolled along loose and sort of sloppy, kept a messy house—but even in a stained blouse and uncombed hair, she stayed the kind of woman who drew men. I think that both scandalized and inspired my mom. Her husband was an alcoholic, and I heard all he ever did at home was sit in his recliner and drink beer until he passed out. I never actually saw that, even though I was interested and kept a sharp lookout when I went to their house.

Mrs. H didn't care one way or another, and my mom loved that.

The Ford suddenly pulled to the side, into a stand of bushes. Branches screeched fingernails on the metal roof. One side of the car sat in sun, the other in shade. Mrs. H reached out her open window, then turned to me in the back seat. She took my hand carefully into both of hers. Skin felt warm on mine, and she left something in my palm.

It was a raspberry. I had never seen one before. I held it up, and it was beautiful. Liquid purple shaded to red in the sun. Mrs. H told me to eat it. My mom started freaking out, and said it might be a poisonous berry, and that you couldn't just pick things off strange bushes by the side of the road and eat them.

"Sure, you can," Mrs. H said. "We're doing that now."

She picked a couple more and gave one to my mom. I think you would have liked them, ghost, in that moment. Two 1960s women, young and pretty, curlers and stretch-slacks, a trace of last night's lipstick, riding through conservative Kansas and determined to change the world. My mom was a rebel, but her friend was—heroic. You would have more than liked them, actually. You would love them, forever.

I know I do.

It felt like two larger than life creatures were debating my fate. Eating the raspberry might get me in trouble, but if I had known the word 'compelled', I would have whispered it to myself, and it would have been exactly the right word.

"You're not a botanist," my mom said. "You could kill everyone in this car."

"I know what a damn raspberry is," Mrs. H said, and I can almost hear the slow, sweet, lazy way she talked. The sweet way she was.

She stretched her arm across the seat and looked back at me. "Go ahead."

I ate it, and it became the most wonderful thing I ever tasted, before or since. Red through and through, warm from the sun, it radiated magic. Something so good grew in plain sight, and hundreds of cars passed and didn't see it. Anybody could pull over, but it stayed invisible, so nobody did. Bushes full of them, and I wanted a thousand, but Mrs. H tugged the steering wheel and pulled us back onto the road, back into the world.

"I don't want to hear you bitch about poison anymore," she told my mom, and they both laughed.

My mom slipped the berry into her mouth, head turned to look out the window so I didn't see her defeat. I feel sad, thinking about it. How sweet it must have tasted; how young she was.

Here's the part I couldn't try to explain, and don't have to with you. Mrs. H pulled off the road to pick one berry and give it to me. It became a lesson, and a treasure, just for me to carry through all the days that were coming. My mom and Mrs. H had their own stories and their own lives, but that doesn't matter because stories can get told side by side, and there are no coincidences. If we all have our small stories, I have mine.

There only needed to be one berry, because eating raspberries wasn't the point. It made a doorway, a lit secret, bubbles in the dark. The pale Ford and the dirt road in Kansas were make-believe. The west behind me had been lost, but there would be other doorways, and that was the message. I'll find my way back to you one day, ghost, even if the map looks like a child's scribbling.

There have been raspberry bushes since then, even if I've passed by without seeing them. There will be other berries.

I can wait.

Dear Ghost,

When we were little, I saw you. Did you know we'd both remember Santa Monica later?

Those Hollywood summers, my mom took me to the pier, or the department store, or swimming lessons, or anywhere that was huge, and she always pointed to something obscure and said, "If we get separated, meet me HERE. Don't forget."

The terrifying thing is, she always picked an ordinary tree with a bench beneath it, or a Sno-Cone cart with bicycle pedals, or a trash basket, or an exit sign. Something completely unremarkable that moved around was best, she thought. If getting lost hadn't occurred to me before, now I was petrified.

Anyway, I woke last night from dreaming something. I sat up and watched the darkness spin—should we have had a plan? Should we have picked a place? A tree with a bench, or an ice cream truck?

You whispered, ghost-warm in my ear—there will be crumbs, remember? If bears are eating them, just follow the bears. They'll be headed for Santa Monica, anyway.

I went back to sleep.

Speaking of department stores, I always liked the mannequins. Not the painted ones, the blank white ones. I looked at the spotless eyes and they moved, just a little, and then everything got colored in and they were people, alive. I knew nobody else saw it. It made me feel weird and happy inside.

I get the same feeling, sitting in the dark and listening to bubbles in a nighttime fish tank. It's a lit doorway to a place I can't find any more, until you come back.

One of these nights, I'll dream I'm too tired to swim any further but I don't know how to stop, and you'll appear from nowhere, floating in a little boat, come to pick me up. You'll hand me a dry towel, poker-faced, like rescuing me is no big deal. Just like every other time you saved me, you'll say.

We'll remember Santa Monica and laugh.

Meet me here.

Dear Ghost,

When I was three, I went to a birthday party for a little boy named Gubber. I remember it like Polaroid: walking through a desert breezeway, carrying the brightly wrapped present that wasn't for me and I wasn't allowed to open. The birthday boy sat on top of a washing machine, watching his guests arrive.

He hit me on the head with a hammer as I passed beneath him. He knocked me down and I had blood in my mouth, so I suppose it was serious.

Just an ordinary claw hammer with a wooden handle, it must have seemed impossibly heavy (at least to the grownups) for such a small boy to swing. I remember that he stayed very calm about it, and so did I. He sat up high watching me, interested. He wore a blue-and-white sailor suit. Everything got very quiet and faded at the edges.

Things became very big and very small, at the same time. Just the two of us, and we watched each other. We were in the Askew, although I didn't know the name for it until much later.

"You can see me," he said. "That means you're going to spend a lot of time alone."

It was a peculiar thing for a small boy to say, but he turned out to be right.

The silence stretched, snapped, and broke into cacophony. My mom screamed and picked me up. The other grownups yelled and rushed in to take the hammer away from Gubber. A nurse at the hospital told me the stitches wouldn't hurt, which was a complete lie. They hurt worse than the hammer, and I finally cried. The scar is still there, even if it's so faded you have to believe in it to see it.

It was kind of a watershed moment, and maybe it formed me. I've stayed calm ever since, both around hammers and the monsters who swing them.

I remembered Gubber today, because when I lined up to check out at the grocery store, a woman squeezed into the space in front of me. I figured she didn't keep track of social distancing and didn't realize I was already waiting my turn. I'm mostly too polite to object to things like that. There's so much else to object to that it seems like a waste of energy, right?

She looked exactly like the Queen of Hearts. The real one, the one Alice knows, not the Disney one. There's no reason I should know what the Queen of Hearts looks like, but I do and I have for a long time. My whole life, I think. Her face and head and mouth seemed enormous, too big by far—but big like you're too close up—do you know what I mean? Take a step back, and the rest of her seemed suddenly small. It's like when you look in a cracked mirror or try on somebody else's glasses.

The queen turned her big head to gaze at me while we waited. She acted pleasant, despite her strangeness. We had a cordial conversation about nothing at all, passing the time. At one point she took my hand and held it between both of hers.

"Do you spend a lot of time alone?" she wondered. "You do, don't you?"

She must have decided then she didn't want to buy anything after all, because she turned and walked away. I hope I never see her again, but I'm sure I will. She's bound to show up in the Askew, sooner or later. No doubt Gubber will, too.

"Did you see that woman I was just talking to?" I asked the man in line behind me. "Didn't she look exactly like the Queen of Hearts?"

He stared at me. "What the fuck are you talking about?"

I had no answer for that. Still, the queen had looked back at me and smiled. She knew I recognized her. It wasn't a nice smile, but perhaps that was my imagination.

The blue-and-green childhood days are never far away, and they draw ever closer as we grow old. The sweet and the strange return to us, like a barely remembered fragrance. The old photographs come back to life, as familiar as bedtime. The monsters come back, too.

Alice knew that—and little by little we do, too.

Dear Ghost,

"Have you ever lost a rental car?" you asked me, once.

Sometimes I wish I had answered you more often, ghost, but your mind usually rocketed to another galaxy and you moved to something else before I could find words. It was never that you didn't listen to me. You listened completely. The answers were in already in my eyes, and my breathing, and you didn't need talk.

I did lose a rental car, in 1983. It happened in Los Angeles, at Disneyland so it was really Anaheim, but that's L.A if you aren't from there.

The month escapes me. I have a weird memory, as you know. Functionally, I'm a mess. I go down to the basement and stand at the bottom of the stairs and wonder why. My mom used to call me the 'absent-minded professor'. I remember details, though—to a degree that people think I'm making them up. I don't know what month I lost the car, though. Maybe because it's always summer in L.A.

Tangent: Remembering that time, I'm listening to Max Webster, 'Let Go the Line'. Did you have that, back in those summers, or was it only for Canadians? Beer and hot streets and back yards and I hated Max Webster, but I loved that song. I still do.

Anyway, I left a rental car in the parking lot at Disneyland, and when I came out it was gone.

Do you know the Jules Verne submarine ride? I had been to Disneyland before, when I was very small. You went down the steps into the submarine and holy shit, there was actual, real water puddled on the floor. The sub vibrated and moved out into the ocean and you pressed your face to the glass. Seaweed swayed and danced. Giant clams gaped open. Everything was lit green, blue, and pink. Mermaids hung in the water-glow outside the windows, waving to you, alive. Bubbles in the dark, right?

I held my dad's hand, and I saw things in the water that he couldn't see. Magic.

Years later it was 1983, and I went on the same ride. I didn't see the same things I saw when I was tiny. The water looked dirty, and the exhausted mermaids adjusted bra straps and didn't try to hide their air hoses. Everything I remembered had been bullshit. I didn't let myself feel sad—that's what growing up normal is, right? Well-adjusted means finding out that everything perfect was just your crazy imagination. Nothing is perfect, and magic and mermaids are no-such-things.

I climbed out of the submarine, and even though I wasn't sad about the loss of baby things, the rest of the day was dark. I couldn't wait to leave and headed for the gates.

In hindsight, I believe if I had scanned the crowds carefully, I would have spotted the Low Gang following me, wearing their dark raincoats, fedora brims pulled low to hide their eyes. I would have seen them flitting from doorways, eating Sno-Cones, slouched in the lineups for rides.

Outside the gates, I couldn't find the fucking car. It wasn't where I left it. Key fobs didn't beep in those days; they were just metal keys that didn't do anything but unlock and start the car—if there was a car, and there wasn't a car. The car was gone.

I rambled the asphalt fields, looked around, rows and rows. I didn't know the license number or anything. I wasn't scared, yet. It gets worse, though, a lot worse. I didn't remember what kind of car it was, or even what color. I don't forget things like that. Remember my weird memory for details? I couldn't recall that car, even though I had picked out and driven it just a few hours before.

The memory makes me nearly sick, even now. The whole thing tastes like nightmare. I didn't know what I was going to tell the rental people. I didn't know how long it would take to walk a hundred miles home to Santa Barbara. When I circled back defeated, the car was sitting right where I'd left it, drab and plain and silver with a Hertz sticker on the bumper.

My hand shook when I put the key in the ignition. I watched the gauges jump to life, turned on the headlights, and drove home.

Here's what I'd say, if I was a writer and I could tell stories, and we both believed in magic. I'd say that submarines and mermaids are always real, and that when I was little I saw things in the water that my dad didn't. I'd say that on that second visit, I decided that it had all been bullshit—and I let the dark in.

There was a collision, underwater on that day in 1983. I decided that mermaids weren't real, and the Low Gang heard me and got a little close for comfort. They took my car, and later they put it back. Because they could, and because they think it's funny when we're confronted with our own definitions of the impossible.

We are born knowing that the Universe is color and light and magic. The un-learning is a gradual thing. By the age of eight we are expected to know that Pizza Hut, arithmetic, and professional football are real, and mermaids are not. We believe in interstate freeways, and that the Moon is a dead rock. We don't believe in other worlds, even though we live in one.

You asked me if I had ever lost a rental car, ghost, but you didn't wait for an answer because it wasn't a question. It was a sticky-note-reminder, a string of crumbs if I get lost. I'll answer you, anyway.

I lost a rental car once, and I believe in mermaids again. I believe in you.

Dear Ghost,

I had such a good dream about you, even though it was in the Askew. I wish I could go back.

It's always nighttime at Askew Beach. I've never arrived during the day, and maybe I wouldn't have the courage to stay there in sunshine anyway. Wood, the smell of creosote, staircases, and railings, all lead down to the dark beach. There are lights; lamps and torches, driftwood fires and paper lanterns, flickering gold and flashing color. People dance on a pier, and their shadows squirm on the sand. Beyond it all the black ocean floats, the vast mother of everything. Painted stars overhead drift behind smoke.

So late. I've come a long way, and I'm tired. I'm always a traveler, because it's what I do and who I am. Dark streets and fluorescent Amtrak stations brought me here. I carry suitcase responsibilities, everything I own, but the heavy luggage is worthless here. I set it down. It will find me again when I leave.

The Askew is forever holiday; strings of bulbs, crowds of people, a kaleidoscope of faces. They ride the roller coaster and line up for the Ferris wheel, play Skee-Ball and shoot balloons. The prizes here are infinite, bright-colored, and transparent. Below me, beach volleyball courts are filled with spread towels, sunglasses and straw hats, people sunning themselves in the starlight. The players leap and twirl, springing and bouncing and stepping in the spaces between towels. Balls arc high and never seem to land.

It all tastes like Seven-Up and smells of coconut oil. Freddie Mercury is shirtless in front of the Tilt-a-Whirl, singing "Love of My Life". The crowd takes up the chorus, every time, which seems to delight him. The Coppertone girl and her little dog wander here, somewhere.

It's summer night, endlessly.

A group approaches. They are not a threat and not particularly hostile, but in every way that matters, they are strange, and strangers. They love you, they know who I am, and I worry them. You belong to them, now.

I show them my empty hands. I'm only a traveler.

"I have somewhere to be," I explain. "I'm trying to catch a train before something catches me. It's chasing me, so I can't stay very long. Have you seen her?"

A woman separates herself and comes close. She reads me with dark eyes and brushes my face with a fingertip, as though she needs to be sure I'm not real. "I know who you're looking for," she says. The kindness in her tone makes my throat tight.

"I've come a long way," I tell her. "I'm very tired."

She unhooks the strap of her bag and rummages. She sets a pair of rubber sandals at my feet.

"You can't go further wearing shoes," she says. "Flip-flops or bare feet. There might not be many rules here, but you can't wear shoes on the beach."

"I have a train to catch," I repeat. "If I take my shoes off, they might not be here when I get back. They won't let me buy a ticket barefoot."

I know what I need to do, but I go back and forth, trying to stay calm. It feels like the dreams where I dial the telephone repeatedly, and always get one digit wrong and have to start over. I look into the woman's eyes for answers. I can't decide and feel sure my heart will bust open because you won't wait for me, ghost.

The woman laughs and refuses to have an opinion, so I know it's really you. You're here.

I bend down, my hands shaking. The laces snap when I untie them, so rotten they fall apart. I realize the shoes are disintegrating too, and it doesn't matter. I'm not going to need them again. I know you waited after all, and I've never been this happy, and

I woke up. I wanted to go back to sleep, but I knew that dreaming and the Askew are two different things, so I came downstairs to make coffee. I held the cup without drinking, and I watched the sky get gray. The early air felt warm. I found a yellow pencil and a piece of paper, and wrote:

'I had such a good dream about you

(Dear Ghost),

even though it was in the Askew. I wish I could go back.'

Dear Ghost

Your first Christmas was my second Christmas, ghost. I got an earlier train, I guess.

We were born into sand, you at tide's edge and me in the desert. They're the same place really; the Mojave only stays barren because it waits for the sea to return. It stands empty, waiting to be filled, and in my heart I always understood that. At night, the desert looks like an ocean. If you stand perfectly still you can hear the faraway rush of water, feel the cool, sense the glinting colors and the return of life.

It's funny how we dismiss our earliest recollections, as if purity doesn't matter. When we were little, we knew for certain all the things they told us later were just imagination. They say it's not normal to have memories as early as we do, and we're inventing them. We smile and agree.

My dad gave me a model railroad that second Christmas. I still waited breathlessly to be a toddler, but he couldn't wait. The train was delicate, grownup, and detailed. My mom laughed and asked what a baby would want with such a thing. The truth is, he gave it to himself, and in hindsight that makes me happy. I don't think he ever got the things he always wanted for Christmas (not when he was a child and not later), and I'm glad if I gave him a reason to open one present for the boy he had once been.

I didn't care about the spidery tracks or the shiny engine that was too heavy for small hands. The red caboose and the tank cars weren't meant for me. I only loved a boxcar. The color of grass, the color of leaves, the color of warm, shallow seas, and green is still my favorite color. A white circle-cross on the side said, 'Santa Fe', and even if I couldn't read, I knew the letters were important. I came from such a place, after all.

The boxcar reminded me of home.

Once, my parents went out, to a party or a nightclub or to dinner, and left me. The people put me to bed. I don't know who they were, but my mom wasn't there, and it wasn't my bed and it wasn't my house. I had my green boxcar that I took everywhere, and they tried to take it away because it had sharp edges (he shouldn't sleep with it—I don't know what they were thinking letting a baby have this in the first place), but I hung on and they gave up and let me keep it. I fell asleep frightened by not-home, but safe in Santa Fe.

Much, much later the world fell out from under me for a while and I slept in dark, strange city places where the only requirement was that I couldn't be found while I slept. I didn't have a green boxcar anymore. I also didn't have a phone number or an address, and I nearly didn't have a name, because nobody knew it. People went on with shopping and eating and talking on the phone. They were in lighted places, and they didn't speak to me. I thought they didn't know how close not-home was to them.

I knew, though. You don't remember where home is until you've been where it isn't.

I got back from a long drive last night, and I stood for a while in the driveway, looking at the sleeping street. Miles of dark highway, rolling through the occasional night-towns that looked like nobody had lived in them for years, unsettled me. I remembered not-home, and I was a little bit afraid, but only for a second. I've been through most of them by now, those strange places. I understand their nature, and they don't bother me much anymore.

I also understand the importance of green boxcars.

When we're very old, I want to sit on wet sand and look at the ocean. There will be lights up the beach, and a string of them far out, beyond the surf. I'll listen like I always do, and when a whistle floats over the water, faint but perfectly clear, I'll look over at you.

"Do you hear a train?"

You'll smile into the dark, and we'll listen some more. Then you'll touch my hand and we'll burst out laughing, because we always knew trains, ever since we were little.

We know what home is, and we're in it.

Dear Ghost,

Last night, I had a Plymouth dream. You were in it, ghost, sitting at your artist table in a long room full of golden lamplight. A dozen mismatched bulbs played with your hair and your smile, like firelight. Paintings flickered on every wall, lingered in corners, and painted eyes watched you. You sat among your crayons and colors, while your printer spit out the years of my letters and the pages of my life.

I promised not to die first, didn't I? Here I am, in dreams.

When I was little, my mom had a 1956 Plymouth Belvedere. She bought it from some guy in Hollywood. She paid a hundred dollars for it. I'm not sure if she ever owned a car before that. It seems like she must have, but I never heard about any others. The idea makes me a little sad and scared because it's a part of her story she took with her, and now I'll never know.

The Belvedere was two-tone, red-and-white, with one rust-colored door that must have come from the boneyard. It had a bullshit odometer, seats like sofas, and it didn't always start. She said she only drove old American cars because they were built better, but the truth is she only had a hundred dollars. That's how she coped with things— saying the tough breaks were just what she always wanted, what she planned in the first place.

(Cars were shit after the '50s. I still believe that, in my heart of hearts, because it's what I believed in 1965. The truths you know when you're little, you know forever.)

I rode across America in the Plymouth back seat, east from Hollywood, away from you. We were already ghosts, you and I, before we even started.

When the old car died, she got a nearly new Volkswagen Beetle. It wasn't American and it wasn't old, but America was giving high school kids guns and sending them overseas to kill children and when the world changed, you dammit-to-hell had to change too. She put flower-power decals on the VW doors and stopped perming her hair. Once at a stoplight a car full of boys whistled at her, and she was outraged but I knew she secretly loved it. She bought a guitar and drove the Beetle to marches.

The bastards threw eggs at her. They didn't see she was practically perfect.

The Plymouth stayed parked in tall weeds beside the driveway and became a spaceship or a fort, depending on the light. I knew garter snakes lived beneath it, even if I never saw one.

Someday, when we're very old, I'm going to sit on night grass and listen to you talk. If there aren't fireflies, we'll know how to make-believe them. I'll stare into warm darkness and remember rolling east when I was little, in the back seat of a Plymouth. I'll feel sad, all over again. You'll read my mind, and your voice will trail off. After a little while, you'll tell me that all the rest of it—all the time since—has been a dream. You were never gone.

I'll watch the fireflies and not say anything but know it's true. You were never gone, and I'll feel better again. Someday.

Dear Ghost,

Most people think ghosts only come out in the dark, but I know different. Ghosts stay in the hours they loved best, and that's where you find them walking. If you're looking.

Once, I had a friend who washed cars all day and led a gang after work. An invisible nobody with his name embroidered over one pocket in sunlight, a barrio prince at night. He took both jobs seriously.

I liked walking to his house after midnight when I needed to hear some wisdom. He gave me cold cans of Budweiser and his wife insisted on feeding me, and they both scolded me for walking by myself into their neighborhood. They said the bad people could see I was crazy and so they let me be, but that wouldn't last forever. I needed to take it seriously, because eventually the bad people would get impatient with my intrusions.

I told them I didn't care, and that was the truth.

She watched me from the stove, and he watched me through cigarette smoke. Their eyes kept me safe. It never occurred to them that they were the bad people, nor did I believe it. I still don't.

They had an ancient Mustang, a V-8 rocket, way too fast, with a top that didn't go up because it had rotted into gray flags. The speedometer didn't work and didn't matter. In the shotgun seat, I put my head back and counted freeway bridges flying overhead. The sky stayed overcast, but the stars came out anyway. The wind blew away sound, felt like it might pull me up and out of the car. I touched my seat belt and wondered what I wished for.

Nobody knew where I was, so nobody could find me, and that can be the safest thing of all.

Off the freeway, we pulled to the curb in front of a church that was getting out, some ritual that ended at one in the morning. Young girls descended stone steps, dressed in white veils. A crowd danced behind them, all wearing masks. To this day, I have no idea what I saw that night. It was magic though, and safe. I remember it sometimes when I'm worried.

Later, we ventured into a better lit part of town, and got the attention of a police cruiser. Headlights bright, blue lights, and my friend stomped the gas and ran. The cruiser eventually dropped back and didn't follow us back into the bad neighborhood, but for a little while it was the strangest thing—an old American car leaking exhaust, leaning hard into turns, worn tires, no carpeting on the floor, my head back on the seat, blue lights flashing behind us.

Safe.

It's funny how the dark can be scary, but most of the times in my life I've been safe have been dark.

I never think about you reading this, ghost, because I'm talking to you years ago (and years from now), but today I'm a shadow whispering echoes, and so are you. Someday there will be the shush of dark surf, footprints in the sand, and I'll walk faster because you'll be just ahead, waiting.

For now, I sleep. I wait, too.

Dear Ghost,

Everything is a Letter, (dear ghost).

Someday when I make you coffee, I'll fold a piece of paper and put it under the cup. There will be rain, and raspberries that you won't eat because they're beautiful. When you see my letter, you'll smile and not read it.

I don't ask for anything because it wouldn't make sense.

(There's already everything.)

Lights in the dark make me miss things I've never seen, if they're beside water.

Once upon a time, Ontario Place sat on the lakefront in Toronto. A huge white cathedral, summer music and fireflies, a fairy tale castle made of spidery catwalks and pods hung out over the water. At night it shimmered with thousands of mermaid lights in glass globes. Staircases and passageways went nowhere, and everywhere. Below, pedal-boats-for-two wandered canals full of underwater lights.

Beyond all of it stretched the lake, vast and black.

It's derelict and forgotten now, but people once strolled and leaned on railings and looked at the glimmering lights against water and sky. In my memory, it's quiet, no matter how many people were there. I always wanted to rent a pedal boat, but I never did. I would have crossed the ocean and be dragging it onto a faraway beach by now, and I think I knew that and it scared me. Even then.

I used to smell the dark air, the summer-at-night, and think: This is perfect.

I want to walk on white catwalks again and feel excited but not hurry. I want to lean on a railing and look at the lights and not say anything at all, except maybe to ask you what color the dark is.

I want to ride in a pedal boat, ghost, on black water, with you.

Dear Ghost,

Wild birds came to you and ate from your palm. I never saw anyone else call birds from the sky, at least not as casually as you did. You fed the dog and then you went outside to feed whatever birds were in the trees, like it was the same thing.

One afternoon, a strange cat sat on top of the fence, dim in the shade of the flowering plumeria tree you loved. He watched you for a little while, tail lashing, and then he launched. He took a feeding dove right off your wrist and disappeared back over the fence. Hours later, I found you kneeling in the same spot. You had given up trying to gather the pieces of your broken heart.

It didn't make sense to you because you were never quite from this world. You loved cats, too.

You told me you'd never feed the doves again.

I wrote you the first letter on September 13, 2012. I talked about being little, and living on Loma Linda Avenue in Hollywood, California.

"When we were little, I saw you."

You told me so, twice. It didn't make any sense because we grew up thousands of miles apart, with most of the Pacific Ocean between us. I already knew you were a little bit strange, maybe the tiniest bit crazy. I put it down to that. I wrote you a letter, anyway.

It was a long letter, because I remembered a lot about the year I turned four. Our house was a Craftsman, shaded by black walnut trees. Most of my memories are cool and pleasant and shady. I don't know why I remember that year so clearly, when most of the later ones are blurred. I imagine I was happy, and at home. I don't know if I've been home since. As I get older, I suspect we eventually go back to the places we love.

Jack Kennedy was newly dead and the Civil Rights Act made headlines, but I didn't know about any of that, or the rest of the smoke over the horizon. I only knew Loma Linda Avenue.

I had a Tonka steam shovel and dump truck, and I found sand under the front veranda, a secret place to play. I learned that if I had a lollipop and was willing to sacrifice it halfway-done, I could use it to call bees. Yellow-and-black appearing from nowhere, crawling on hard blue candy. It glowed magic until I got my first sting. I realize, writing this, that the white-hot pain and the betrayal was my first adult experience. My mom made it better with baking soda mixed into a paste. She had her own magic powders.

A pretty good tricycle sat in the driveway with my name on the registration, but I felt outraged I couldn't have a bicycle. I wanted a big one, not a kid's bike. My dad said I was still too small. Half a century later, that still sounds like bullshit, Dad.

A guy named Tony lived in the little garage apartment behind the house. He wore white t-shirts and smoked Camel cigarettes. Years later, I saw the Fonz on television and felt startled, like I knew him. Tony had a motorcycle painted metal-flake, magic sparkles floating beneath deep green. My mom thought the motorcycle would fall off its kickstand every time I went to look at it, and she yelled from the kitchen window. I wondered how she knew, every single time, and if she just stood there all day watching me. She let Tony take me around the block some evenings, though. I sat in front on the gas tank, holding on for dear life. I remember the wind and the roar, freedom, lights in Hollywood dusk, and I suspect he took me farther down Santa Monica Boulevard than my mom thought. Magic takes hold early, if it takes hold at all. I've chased those rides ever since.

A monster with a bald head wandered the back yard, and sometimes a Santa Claus with no head sat laughing in one of the metal chairs on the veranda. My dad said I dreamed them and sometimes people with a good imagination couldn't tell the difference between real life and dreams. I didn't see why there had to be a difference, and I still don't. Monsters don't have to be real to be true.

Mostly I remember my mom, young and fierce and pretty. She was small, and she drove an enormous Plymouth Belvedere because she liked big American cars. We battled over the things I wouldn't eat and the things I wouldn't do, and she made the center of the universe. I didn't know I wouldn't have her for long.

The Goodyear blimp floated outside my bedroom window some nights, lonely and terrifying and beautiful, filming the Dodgers. Candy bought on Saturday afternoons had to be saved for after supper. Tiny sips of my dad's drink when he watched baseball, and my parents laughed at the face I made. I remember a little girl watching me—something to do with ice cream—and I never forgot her dark eyes.

So I wrote my letter and wondered if it was a story. I wondered if I loved you.

I didn't find out for years that you and your mom lived in Hollywood for one year, the year you turned four. I looked on a map, and you lived around the corner from our house on Loma Linda. Then you moved away, and we moved away, and the Universe would need decades to bring you back. A little dark-eyed girl, and even as a toddler you knew there are no coincidences.

When we were little, I saw you.

Dear Ghost,

You told me once that when you were little, you wanted to know what was inside of things. A door might be made of wood, but what was inside the wood? And when your mom said molecules, you instinctively grasped the idea and probably pleased her—but what was inside of that?

I think perhaps you stood then, a toddler in bare feet, toes curled, and peeked over the edge of the universe.

They've told you to close your eyes, ghost, ever since. Look at sports cars, stock options, and fashion shows— like normal people. Fix a drink and find you some well-adjusted. Mark Helprin once said, "I have been to another world, and come back. Listen to me." You listened and you remembered, even if you did your best to be agreeable and forget.

I rescued a photo from the trash, or rather caught it on the bounce after somebody else did. It was once a gift, opened. There are tiny bits of tape and orange wrapping paper on the back. It never had the plastic film removed, and it never got hung on anyone's wall. A moment caught, memorialized, gifted, and then discarded.

I wonder if it was too unimportant to keep, or too painful. I picked it up, mostly because you would have. We both like lost things—you've been a dancing ghost and I've hitchhiked in the middle of the night, and we know what lost is.

Now the image will hang, slightly askew, in this strange room, here among dreams.

It compels me, and it makes me uneasy. Mexico or South America, I think. Nine horses, moving fast. A parade for grim bystanders. Three women, six men. Four bare heads, five wearing fedoras. Faces with the hard set of people who have seen hard things and never talk about them. I don't know what the numbers mean, only that I've seen this place before and it isn't Mexico or South America. It's a place called Askew, and you showed me how to get there, the first time.

I heard a tiny noise behind me just now, a small splash. Some instinct made me turn and go to hands and knees, shine a light under the bookcase. The minnow went from floor back to aquarium in the palm of my hand. A bare minute of gasping, and he's gone back to his life and he doesn't remember me, and that's how the universe works. He's none the worse, except for a couple of long white hairs that trail his swimming like conquistador banners.

The strange thing is, I felt your hand on my shoulder just as I heard the splash. Don't the dead turn up in the strangest places?

That's how the universe works, too.

Dear Ghost,

When I was little, we went to San Diego to see the pearl divers. That might not have been the only reason, (I know there were Volkswagen Beetles and supermarkets, and my mom clipped a bow tie at my neck and put Old Spice cream in my hair) but it turned out to be the reason that still matters. All these years later, everyone is long gone and it's the place I go, to wait for them. The pearl diver place.

I remember wet cement and echoes and it costs a dollar. Everyone is talking loud and moving around, shorts and sleeveless dresses and the smells of beer and cigars and sweat. My dad points and I lean into a metal railing and it all goes—silent. Cold and salt and black water, and I see her a long way off. Coming, but in no hurry.

She swims up (surfaces young-and-old, with dark eyes I'll never forget, and her smile is solemn like she knows everything) and she palms my plastic token and gives me back an oyster, so rough it shocks my skin. It's heavy and ugly and beautiful, and it's—revelation.

She treads water and watches my face, to make sure I understand.

Then she dives, and I'm supposed to keep the oyster because it's strange and perfect and it came from her, but it's taken away with smiles before I can even get to know it. My sudden tears as the man cuts it open with a knife, and my mom shows me a black pearl, nestled in her palm.

Somehow, I understand it isn't what she expected, and she doesn't really want it, but it's too late.

The diver was a mermaid. I understood it then, and I understand it now. I forgot, for a while in the middle, when I got lost in the real world. I've looked for her, and my oyster, without knowing I was.

Mermaids, however dark and frightening, generally know where green oranges grow. They teach us how to climb and pick them. Green oranges are like tangerines from far away, and we remember the taste even if it's our first time. If we're lucky the mermaid will take us back down with her when the time comes, because everyone goes to Askew Beach, sooner or later. Everyone wades into the dark surf, and when the water reaches our waist, we're not coming back.

All the silly things were silly, all along. We have to give them back, and they float behind us for a moment before a wave takes them.

During the day, there will be blue water, the ocean not far away, and hot sun on green hills. Trees grow inside, brush the ceilings out of the way, and the sound of breezes turning the pages of forgotten books will be the same as the leaves moving overhead. Ice and spices, running water, dogs chasing fish, you laughing.

You show me green oranges, mermaid, and how to climb and pick them.

At night the stars outside are purple-white, but lamps inside turn all the colors into shades of gold. There are no doors, so spaces melt together. The breeze can get cool, so you keep a jacket on your chair, just in case. The things that have been perfectly broken, the things nobody else wants or even sees, curl up at your feet. The water still runs after nightfall, but the fish are invisible now, floating in mid-dark.

You have popcorn in a green bowl (and dark eyes). I remember you.

Sleep.

Dear Ghost,

Our dog barks at the front door. It's called a Dutch door, and I open the top half.

A young woman stands on the step, holding a leash. The strange dog at the other end is young, not quite a puppy, but she hasn't reached her size yet. Both of these visitors are teenagers, I suppose. The woman seems a little vague, as though someone just woke her from a nap. She looks like the people who emerge from dark movie theaters and stand blinking in the sun for a moment.

"She isn't mine," she says, and gestures to the pup. "I took her."

"I see," I say, but I don't.

"They beat her. My neighbors. She's just a puppy, and I couldn't listen to her screaming any more. I guess I stole her."

Her clothing is cotton, and comfortably wrinkled. The shirt is printed with tiny flowers.

"Then you rescued her," I offer, carefully, because I've stepped in quicksand before. "That isn't exactly stealing."

She shrugs. "I can't keep her—not right next door. Some lady said I should bring her to this address. She can live here, now. She'll be safe."

"You got the wrong address," I say. "What lady?"

"The lady who lives here," she says. "I guess."

I start to tell her that no lady lives here, not anymore. I stop because part of me still believes that isn't true. She holds out the leash loop, and I take it because I don't know what else to do. I open the door the rest of the way.

"The lady said you'd take good care of her," the woman says. "You're good with dogs, she told me."

"I'll take care of her," I promise, which is absurd. This is a stolen dog. I feel your warm breath on my ear, ghost, and at once I know the dog will never go back where she came from. She lives with us, now.

"What did the lady look like?" I ask.

The young woman shows me an elaborate shrug.

"See you later, mister."

I watch her retrace steps to the street. She doesn't look back. No car waits at the curb for her. I don't know if she came here on foot, or perhaps has a ride waiting around the corner, out of sight. In any event, she is another rainbow, one who will loom important for the briefest moment, and then disappear from my story.

Once inside, I remove the leash. The young dog's collar is studded with small spikes. After a moment I remove that, too. The three of us make our way back to the kitchen and the water bowl. My dog's half-eaten bowl of kibble gets devoured. He doesn't mind.

We head for the back yard and a before-lunch snooze. The puppy takes the bed you set under the umbrella. Our dog sprawls beside her, unconcerned even though he's slept in it since he was very small. He doesn't mind that, either. He's a good boy. The two of them are asleep, nearly instantly. I wonder if we already have a routine, the three of us.

"Bye for now," you whisper.

"Don't go too far," I murmur back.

After a little while, I fall asleep too.

Dear Ghost,

I dream about suitcases, lately. Maybe that's what getting old and wise means—emptying drawers of memories to decide what's worth taking. If you're smart, you fold a few things carefully and leave the rest strewn across the floor. Walk out and don't look back.

Glance up at the clock from time to time for me, dear ghost. I don't know what time my train leaves, but I think I know where I'm going. I'll end up on the Santa Monica Pier, during the summer of 1963.

I tell the conductor when I get on, and he smiles when he punches my ticket because he already knows. That's where I came from, after all—so it makes sense I'll go back. I see smog, and L.A smells like sweat, cigars, and baby oil—but the ocean looks exactly the same.

We lived in Hollywood when I was little, and that's the place you've gone to wait for me.

Our house is a Craftsman with a big front porch. A couple of black walnut trees grow in the front yard and keep things shady. I see you now, on the front steps. A book opens on your lap, and a small breeze plays with your hair. You sit quietly, wearing peach-and-green and watching things nobody else sees. When the wind shifts, you disappear.

Dead battery, the walnut trees whisper. She has to find a charger, that's all. Wait.

A granny-flat apartment stands over the garage in back. A guy named Tony and his wife stay there (they aren't really married, and nobody will rent to them if they get found out). Tony wears white t-shirts and straight jeans, and a black leather jacket when he rides his motorcycle. He's a hoodlum, but my mom really likes him. He and his friends are her age, nicer and more fun than the people she knows, and it makes her wistful, sometimes.

We have rats. Big rats, the wharf kind. They scamper in the walls at night, and the dogs go crazy, scratching at the plaster. Tony's girlfriend walked through the garage one day, carrying a bag of groceries, and a rat dropped down from the rafters and bit her. My parents stand beneath the kitchen window, talking.

—Oh my God, what would that rat do to a child? We should move.

—Don't worry, that woman loves attention, she drinks and exaggerates, rats don't attack people.

I ride my green pedal car around the paved courtyard in front of the garage. One afternoon, a huge rat walks out and sits down. He doesn't say anything, and neither do I. We look at each other for a while, but no one comes. I get out of the car and walk softly to the house. I stay quiet and close the back door behind me. The rat never moves.

We aren't finished, the two of us. He was a letter for me. Unopened, he's still there, the rat, and so am I.

I have a metal construction set to play in the sand—dump truck and bulldozer and steam shovel. I also own a Tonka garbage truck, with a square hole in the back to stuff with imaginary garbage. One day I put some bright-colored gumdrops in the hole, and bees come. I've drawn a spell, and my conjured spirits fly in and out of the truck. They crawl over my fingers, even prettier than the candy. Black and yellow, blue and pink, absolute magic until the stinging starts and doesn't stop. I feel my screams now, remembering.

I pour my frosted flakes right to the top of the bowl every morning, because that's the way the tiger does it on TV. Make a nice little mountain in the center, then spill milk carefully and leave me alone, I don't need help. The cereal has to be crispy, just kissed by milk, but after a couple bites it starts to get soggy and I'm done. It's a waste and starving children would love to eat mush. Morning after morning, my parents yell and take turns trying to get me to pour less or eat more. They even put the mess in the fridge and serve it to me for dinner.

I cry, but I won't budge. I can't, because I can't.

I will always persist about those things that matter, my whole life. Frosted flake promises and your smile, ghost. I won't forget you, and I won't be turned back. I have a crew cut, my first, and some goopy stuff to rub in my hair. It's for grownups, OLD SPICE. A sea rover under full sail on the jar and it smells funny—but it's potion. The pirate fragrance is the spell that will carry me west, back home, one day.

I was little once, in Hollywood. I remember.

The Goodyear blimp floats by my bedroom window at night, flashing colored lights, all at once terrifying and beautiful and lonely.

Like us.

Dear Ghost,

My mom wakes me up, in the middle of the night.

Let's go. Just put on the shorts you wore today.

My parents fought all day, and it had been a bad one, maybe the worst ever. Doors got slammed, things got thrown, shouts got broken, and I went to sleep in a damp cloud of divorce. Now I follow my mom to the door, scared. My dad waits for us, outside. He watches something up the street, and he won't look at us.

We start walking. It's after midnight, and I always wanted to be up this late and never imagined going outside.

I don't know where we're going. Summer, and the night feels as warm as day, the kind of dark air that makes everything smell and sound like it's a secret. Bright sidewalk, and invisible night things parallel-walk us in the shadows, moving porch-to-porch and bush-to-tree, keeping time with us.

Then out onto the ocean boulevard, where the traffic flows and the sidewalks burst with people wearing flip-flops and safari hats. The hush of surf moves beneath all the spinning light. I didn't know this went on every night while I slept, these happy people who live in a midnight world.

Don't walk way back there, my mom calls. *Walk with us.*

Her voice is stern, but her face stays a little shy. I run to catch up and have to walk in the middle so I'm not choosing between them. Looking back, I know that's what they both wanted.

We three, walking.

At the amusement park entrance: Colored lights and saltwater taffy, and the roller coaster roars and hurtles over our heads, as loud as a plane crash. People carry stuffed animals and waxed cups of Coca-Cola. From speakers mounted high on poles, Glen Campbell insists he's a rhinestone cowboy, over and over.

I'm a little wistful, but that isn't what tonight is about and we don't turn into the park. I don't know what tonight is about, but my parents talk to each other over my head and I see the faintest, awkward beginnings of smiles. The smiles aren't meant for me, but I sense that I'm somehow making them possible, and that feels good. Better than good.

I keep quiet, watch everything and say nothing. Like now.

Past the park, it gets a little quieter and a miniature golf place is open. My dad says lucky he brought his wallet, and we go to the window. I'm so excited—I can't believe this is happening. We each get a putter. Mine is heavier than I expect, and I don't know what to do.

My dad shows me the right way to hold it, fingers just so. He handles his with the extraordinary grace he uses to field a baseball or toss a football, like it's all a part of him and he is weightless. Nothing in my experience prepares me for my mom being a star, though. She leads us around tiny windmills and gaping crocodile mouths, sinking impossible putts and showing how golf gets done when you're made from moon dust.

I see the surprise on my dad's face. He hadn't known she could do this, either. I think he wonders what other wonders he might not know about. After a while, he forgets about his own game because he only wants to watch her.

The game ends, because everything does. A slow meander back the direction we came from, but there's soft ice cream and we sit together on a stone wall to eat it. A black dog wanders up, and my mom tells me to only pat his head because there are places with missing fur and I shouldn't touch him there. He can't come with us, she says, because the street is his home. Her face is inexpressibly sad. It's hard, but that's the way things are sometimes.

Maybe she knew she was telling me about myself, ghost. Maybe she knew I would need to know that, someday.

She takes my dad's wallet and disappears for a few minutes. When she comes back, she has a hamburger wrapped up in paper. She gives it to the dog, the whole thing, with certain ceremony. It's just for him, and she won't divide meat and bun. I ask her if it has ketchup and she says yes. I tell her I didn't know dogs ate ketchup, and she says this one does, and looks sad again.

I don't remember the end. I don't remember walking back, and I don't remember going to my bed and sleep. I remember everything else, but the end is a huge blank. That used to seem strange, but now I understand.

There never was an end. That night is still going on. My mom and dad are still playing miniature golf in the dark, and she's still beating him. The black dog is home now, and hers.

You are colored lights in a dark sky, ghost. I see them up close, even though I'm far away.

You're a doorway back to what I'm trying to remember, and to where I've never been before. It's why I see you little and very old at the same time. I remember you as a toddler, but when you glance my way, the wind plays with your gray hair.

It's raining on the Moon right now, and I miss you.

Dear Ghost,

You told me once that magic spells can only be written with a yellow pencil—not dull but not sharp—or they don't work. You touched my forehead to make sure I was listening.

So, I'll draw a treasure map with a yellow pencil, on a scrap of paper torn from a calendar that hung in someone's kitchen before I was born. I'll fold it carefully and tuck it into a Roi-Tan cigar box, with green feathers, seashells, and bits of colored glass from a broken kaleidoscope.

A girl I'll never meet will find it years from now, on her birthday. She'll touch the shells with bare fingertips and unfold the little map. She'll be flooded with a peculiar feeling, sad-and-happy, and not know what it means. Her heart will read my map just fine, though.

Outside a small town in Canada, buildings end and the pavement turns to gravel. I'm eleven, and I drop my bike at the edge of the woods and walk. The road bends left, and behind a dense screen of trees a house stands, burned so long ago the thick stone walls are washed clean and the rooms are carpeted with grass. There's a brook running through the remnants of backyard, and raspberry bushes are heavy with purple and red. The house is warm with ghosts who love me. Only you can see this place, boy, they say.

A secret, and it's all just starting. Someday I'll live here.

I'm fifteen and walking a little bit lost, on a dirt road in a place called Murrell's Inlet in South Carolina. Shade so deep it's black is draped with Spanish moss. A closed shack sits in the cool, selling Budweiser and bait. Through the trees, I see hot sun, bright water, and the orange-and-white flank of a fishing boat. My feet are bare, the dirt feels good, and I smell shrimp and hush puppies. The ghosts here haven't seen a stranger in years.

I'm not a stranger, though. I know this secret place, and it's all just starting.

One o'clock in the morning and walking Toronto sidewalks is better than trying to sleep. Summertime, and my heart is broken at twenty. I don't know yet that cracked hearts don't ever heal, not really, not if they've been broken right. The bars overflow onto the streets, music and colored lights running into the gutters. The people are beautiful, and everyone has fun. They always have full wallets and know exactly what to do. Nobody's heart is busted.

I'm a gray-and-green phantom. The beautiful people can't see me, but someday I'll be beautiful too. It's all just starting.

One day the birthday girl will open my map, but I'll be somewhere else by then. Night surf, yellow moonlight, my pants wet to the knees, and I'm walking again. I empty my pockets and scatter everything I've ever truly owned on the beach: green feathers, seashells, and bits of colored glass from a broken kaleidoscope.

We're not lost, ghost. I don't need a map now because I'm following your bare footprints in the sand. It's all just starting.

Dear Ghost,

Seeing you again will be the end of a picture show. It's silly to be afraid of it, you insist. Open your eyes.

The curtain comes so fast, I wonder if I dozed off. The credits roll, and people around me are already on their feet, slipping into slipped-off shoes and checking their seats for fallen-out things. Others aren't ready to go. The lights come up but they sit frozen, staring at the screen and carefully avoiding eye contact, as if reading "costume-supervisor-location-manager-sound-mixer" makes a charm, a spell that will keep The End from being the end.

I've never waited for the end of anything. I head up the aisle, to whatever comes next.

On the way in, the lobby was kaleidoscope, bright lights, and excitement. Now it's hushed, dim enough to say there won't be more showings tonight—at least not for me. A couple of employees in pastel vests cast polite eyes my way, to make sure I'm headed toward the exit.

Stiff from sitting, and so tired my eyes hurt, I see night outside the entrance.

The snack bar is closed, and the languid teenaged faces behind it are busy, covering and wiping things down. The smell of buttered popcorn lingers, but its fragrance is empty. The promises of Milk Duds and Coca-Cola don't mean much now, and I can't remember why I lined up for them.

It occurs to me I feel the same way about meaningless sex and big houses and red Ferraris. I remember the wanting, but not the why.

I push through the glass doors to the sidewalk. You wait outside the glow of marquee lights, watching traffic. Hair tucked behind your ear, the softer illuminations of taillights and neon signs color your face. You glance at me. Your eyes talk, and there's no way I could have held the memory of how beautiful you are. I knew you'd be here, but the warmth fizzing in my chest is strange and almost more than I can contain.

The night air feels good; soft and warm. I'm still breathing, because why wouldn't I be breathing here, and I'm glad it's summer. It's what I hoped for. I smell city—perfume and exhaust, cigarettes and food—and the fragrances are just the same as always. I hear the whoosh of cars, the murmur of unseen crowds, and Blondie sings "Heart of Glass" from a rooftop.

The best things are eternal because there are no accidents and no coincidences. I want to kiss you, but not yet. We have time, now.

"How was your movie?" you ask. "Did you have fun?"

I nod and shrug, at the same time. "Mostly okay, I think. I'm not sure about fun." I haven't really had time to think about the show being over, and forever beginning.

"Tell me the truth." Your laugh makes me laugh too, the way it always did. "You thought the movie was all there was, didn't you? They told you nothing was real, and you believed it."

It seems foolish now, with this never-ending city blooming around us, but maybe I doubted magic. Some dark mornings, I thought dreams were only synapses. I shrug again.

"We should go for pie," you confide. "Find a diner and sit in a booth. It isn't really a date, if we don't."

"I always wanted to get pie and coffee after a movie," I say. "Hold hands under the table and talk about the show."

"No sense, otherwise." You nod. "Romance was always the point."

I move to cross the street, and you touch my elbow. Look. A paper-girl glides past, jangling her bicycle bell. On the opposite corner, an old woman watches us. She holds a duck in the crook of one arm. There are Christmas lights in the trees, which is perfect in our July. We never believed in rules.

"Afterward, we can walk down to the lake," you say. "It's a nice walk, if you're not too tired."

I catch your hand. I'm walking with you as long as you'll have me, and I tell you so. I'm not tired, anymore.

Your breath is warm against my ear. "They run the Ferris wheel all night here," you murmur. "Let's go."

Dear Ghost,

When I write to you, I sit down at the piano and play a couple of notes. I hang them in the dark air, like lights. Then I wait.

I'm afraid of not being home. Sometimes when I'm checking out library books, sitting at work, cruising the grocery store, paying bills, or riding my bike on streets and blocks I've known for decades, I watch faces and think—I don't know these people. How did I get here, to this strange place? I'm not supposed to be here. We must have stopped for gas in the middle of the night, and I went to the bathroom and my parents just drove off and now I live here, in this middle-of-the-night gas station.

I'm more afraid of calling somewhere home, just because it's where I am. I sleep in a dark place, covers over my head, when I have miles and miles to travel. So scared I'll grow old believing that keeping my eyes closed is safe—safer than wind blowing tears, colored lights flashing by, going back to where I belong.

I stay afraid of dying without ever having remembered how to fly.

In the winter of 1982, I got off a bus in Santa Barbara, because the ocean stopped me. I would have gone further west, if I could. I didn't know anyone. I had no money, no job, nowhere to stay, and I wasn't afraid. I loved all of it. I was west.

Always alone, but never alone. I knew you, ghost, and I talked to you—even before I touched your face or said your name. The beach felt dangerous at night, and it enchanted me. I went to watch the surf in the dark, spreading white on black sand, away from lights. I wasn't home yet, but I was on my way. I believed that everything hard is just an adventure.

I liked to go to a movie theater on lower State Street. An early ticket and I sat for a while, quiet and empty, before the movie started. Balconies hung above me, lit up soft gold. A make-believe village somewhere, probably Mexico, and the kids and dogs had been called in for the night. Everyone making dinner and they didn't know I was there, watching them from the dark. They didn't know they were real.

With my head on the back of the seat, I looked up at the stars in the ceiling, tiny sparks in a warm black sky. A jewelry box spill on velvet, you said later, and watched my face to see if I understood.

When the people filed in, deciding where to sit, the curtains rolled back and 'COMING ATTRACTIONS' played on the screen, I got up and left. I wasn't there to see a movie—I was there to be home for a little while.

You were the coming attraction.

Sometimes, I believe in you. I sit down at the piano and play a couple of notes. I hang them in the dark air, like lights. Then I wait.

Dear Ghost,

I think a lot about baseball.

It makes no sense, maybe, because I'm not even sure who won the World Series this year. I can't remember the last game I watched on television, and I don't check the box scores these days. It's a mark of getting old, I guess, that game-winning home runs and crushing the opposing pitcher don't appeal to me anymore. I don't want to end anyone's dreams. There's been enough of that. I'd as soon get to the end without causing more hurt, if I could.

Eleven was yesterday.

Our Little League park sits on the corner, laid out so home plate faces away from traffic. Cars are pulled onto the grass. Parents hang off chain links. The umpire struts and waves, hurrying to get in nine innings before the fireflies come out. We'll play into dusk if we have to because Little League is serious. The dry outfield still smells of the hot day, of summer ghosts.

The coach taps my shoulder. His mouth turns down, like he has no choice. The bat gets heavier as I walk to the plate. Just getting there is overwhelming. It seems like enough heroics.

The opposing pitcher is a mean kid named Steve. He goes to a different school than me. He's lights-out, a prodigy, the best athlete in the league. His blue jersey is tucked in, his cap squared. He isn't one of those long-haired golden-boy athletes, effortlessly good at everything, including friends and girls. I heard he doesn't even talk to his own teammates.

Steve isn't in this for girls. He's in this for the batters. This little ballpark is a brief stop on the way to All-America, to places none of the rest of us will ever see.

I'm a guaranteed strikeout, a box to be ticked, as interesting as using a dustpan after the floor is swept.

"Guaranteed," the catcher calls, and tosses Steve the ball.

My uniform is red-and-white. My mom washes it after every game. I wish she wouldn't get rid of the occasional grass and dirt stains. They might prove that I'm a player, that I belong here, that I might lash out a single on the very next pitch. A little mud might make me belong.

My only hope is a walk on balls, so I leave the bat on my shoulder. Fat chance.

The ball comes so fast I can't even see it. Steve isn't bothering with drama—three down the middle like he's tossing warmup. The umpire yells, "Three!" like it doesn't matter. I walk back to the dugout. I wasn't expecting anything else, but my eyes sting because nobody is even looking at me. I didn't know I was quite so invisible.

Steve won't play baseball after his junior year in high school. They push his elbow too hard in Little League, and by the time he has his driver's license throwing a fastball makes his arm swell. He gets by on baseball smarts for a little while, but the batters get better and better. They routinely chase him after a couple of innings, so he's done.

Guaranteed.

Steve will turn into a silent man, one who looks perpetually angry and cheated. He'll drive a plumber's truck for the rest of his life. Only the Chevy vans with writing on the sides will change, getting newer as he gets older. A dump truck is going to run a light to demolish the last one, and Steve will be gone before he turns fifty. I might be the only one from Little League who remembers him, these days.

In the end, we're all guaranteed.

I'll know I'm gone when I move with a crowd along a concourse. Brick walls are hung with banners, and above them the sky is hung with the pink clouds that mean early summer. A man screams, "Prooooo-grams! Pro-GRAMS!" like he's broken.

Past metal turnstiles, I move through old cement and iron columns, swept along by the echoing footsteps made by ten thousand pairs of shoes. The letters and numbers painted on brickwork, black-and-white, look as though they were done with a brush a century ago. It's dark like a weird cathedral. When I see Gate 5-78, I feel my heart beat and I'm happy and surprised it's still there.

The far end of the tunnel opens into sudden light and green, green grass. It's all clean and beautiful. The crowd noise swells. The bright-uniformed players are immediate, both tiny and impossibly close. Pennants flutter from light standards. The banks of bulbs are lit even though the sun hasn't gone down.

You wave frantically to me from halfway along a row. You point to the empty seat next to you. I nod and do my best to look cool, but I can't keep my poker face. I hear your laughter when my silly grin busts out. You have a hot dog with mustard waiting for me in a cardboard tray, but I'm too happy to eat anything. You're balancing two cold Coca-Colas, so I take one. It comes in a red-and-white cup that reminds me of my Little League uniform, but that doesn't make me sad. Not anymore.

I'm pulled down into my seat, and you lean into me, warm. You smell like everything good. We won't watch the game because we have too much to talk about. Forever won't be long enough.

Guaranteed.

Dear Ghost,

Letters to you are music. I sit here in the dark, touch a couple of notes, and listen for echoes. I find the black keys work best. Sometimes I don't hear anything at all, but other times colors blossom and you're there.

I remember being little, but I also remember being very old. That's crazy, I know—as crazy as spending most my life looking for someone I saw once when I was a toddler, without knowing I was doing it. As crazy as actually finding you.

At three in the morning, an ancient guy with an attitude looks at me from the bathroom mirror, and I wonder how the hell I ever got to be a hundred, like something out of a damn storybook. You told me once that time is a map, and if I learned to read the road behind me, I'd be able to read the road ahead. Maybe when I see myself old, I'm just reading your map.

I dream about a birthday party—your 98th. There's ice cream and music, and you laugh and tell me I'm in charge of the fireflies.

When I was one, I almost drowned in a bathtub. That's another story, but not this one.

My mom never met a crisis that couldn't be met with a crazy counter-attack. She decided I might try again, so I needed baby swimming lessons. That was before 'water babies' and all sorts of other modern things that have come and gone. In those days, learning to read before you were five didn't happen. Everybody got married when they turned twenty-one. Nobody threw babies in a swimming pool.

Undaunted, my mom found a lady named Shirley who taught babies to swim. I know we had to drive a long way to get there, once a week. Her sitting up straight behind the huge steering wheel, a red-and-white 1957 Pontiac Star Chief, and I liked to stand up beside her and hold onto the seat back. She made me sit down over and over, like that kept me safe.

She was enough to keep me safe, but she wouldn't be there for very long.

There was an airport on the way, and it was my favorite thing. (She told my dad, and he said maybe I would be a pilot.) It was only for small planes, and there were parked lines of Cessna and Piper, all the same white, but with different color stripes. Crayons.

After my lesson, we always got an ice cream sandwich, because that was both our favorite thing. It was our moment, our towel-and-wet-hair shared secret. We never had ice cream sandwiches otherwise, and we never had them later—just when I was a toddler, after baby swimming lessons.

I've liked ice cream sandwiches ever since, but I never knew why until you came along and reminded me. There are good secrets and bad ones. The good secrets are kept sometimes, like promises, so ice cream is a doorway to all the things I've lost.

I remember one day in particular. I close my eyes and play a couple more notes and I'm there.

The pool is aqua and so bright with sun that I have to squint. I want to be sure I can see before I go under, but Shirley submerges me before my eyes are ready, so I cry. I'm not afraid of the water—I'm mad. She wants to do it again—onetwothreeBobby—but fuck her, you know? I cry harder.

Shirley tells my mom that I won't cooperate today, and maybe it's best not to force it. They agree I had been doing so well and it's too bad. My mom is embarrassed but she stays very sweet and polite and keeps her poker face.

In the car on the way home, we pass the airport and I happily point out the planes all lined up. (I can see them right now.) I'm standing up again, but she isn't making me sit down. She tells me that we aren't getting ice cream because I cried. That was the deal we had, Bobby. If you don't cry, if you're GOOD, you get ice cream after. We'll try again next week.

I'm bewildered. Our thing has nothing to do with swimming, nothing to do with Shirley. We pass the ice cream sandwich store, and I turn backward to watch it disappear in the rear window.

Lives turn on a dime, and I think mine would have turned out differently if that had been the end. It might have been easier, better-ordered, more goal-oriented. I might have learned an important, valuable lesson that day. I might be sitting now in a luxury condominium looking at travel brochures, instead of sitting here in the dark, writing letters to a ghost. Life is a hell of a lot easier without magic.

I do know I inherited one thing from my mom more surely than anything else—a granite exterior and a marshmallow heart.

We turned into a big supermarket parking lot, a strange one we didn't go to. She got me out. All the way in back, the ice cream freezer had a glass door that let out a breath of frosted cold when it got opened. She was carrying me and had to lean inside. The woman at the register smiled at me while my mom fumbled coins.

That day was even better than usual because my mom wasn't sure if she was doing the right thing giving it to me when she said she wouldn't. She had broken a good-parent vow. She wanted it too, though. The ice cream didn't matter as much as having deepened the secret. If we were bad, we were bad together. Sweet.

I hope wherever she is now, my mom knows that breaking the rules that day probably saved me. I hope it makes her smile, remembering.

A couple of years later, I was still little when I first saw you, ghost. Solemn and dark-eyed, you held your mom's hand and watched me. That was about ice cream too, and I never forgot you and never stopped looking for you. I have a feeling I was seeing you not for the first time, but— again. Maybe your map shows past lives and other worlds, too.

I need to sleep, so I close the cover on the piano. I see fireflies. I see night sky, and lit colors. It's warm.

Happy ninety-eighth, ghost. You're going to be beautiful.

Dear Ghost,

You told me once that you talked too much, and I was puzzled because you usually stayed shadow-silent and barely spoke at all. You explained that you told me everything in your head, walked through your days talking to me, and I just needed to hold still and listen. That's why I move quietly through noisy places these days. You have too much to tell me to ever be gone.

When I was thirteen, I had a poster taped to my bedroom wall. Posters were a big deal then, rolled up and wrapped in plastic: Farrah Fawcett or Barbi Benton, running horses, the 1974 Boston Red Sox, early Freddie Mercury. The best poster stores were on Yonge Street, jumbled messes jammed between head shops and all-day-all-night live sex shows. We went there in our school uniforms and sneakers, wide-eyed on grimy sidewalks, hopeful some of the filth would cling to us when we left.

In my case, I guess it did.

I only had one poster, on purpose. I understood even then that magic can be diluted, that spells can go pale and disappear. So just the one over my bed, taped carefully at the corners. The poster was the kind that unrolled white, but dense with black lines that made no sense. It needed to be scribbled with markers, over the course of hours and days. Bringing it to life depended on careful consideration and choice of colors.

A blimp floated over a forest toward an improbable mountain with a castle perched on the side. One horizon was summer, with masted sailing ships on a distant ocean. Shy mermaids lounged on rocks, and green dolphins leapt beneath wheeling gulls. On the other horizon night sky spun, filled with dark rainbows and planets and faraway worlds.

In between was everything else. I lay on my bed and looked at the places that waited for me.

When I find my way back to you, when it's time to go, I won't board an airship—at least not at first. I'll shrug on a backpack and head for the bus. I walked all these grimy sidewalks and learned to see in the dark for a reason, after all. There will be dangerous places and long nights to travel through when I start out. I know that now.

The old L.A Greyhound station at the corner of East 6th and Los Angeles Street is closed for good, but it still marks the end of the world. If you want to see where all the clocks stop, I'll take you there.

If you look at the poster on my bedroom wall long enough, the place is still open.

It's always night, always busy, and it's hard to tell the good monsters from the bad. Burly security men pace and impose mad king authority—no smoking, no drinking, no sleeping on the plastic benches. They keep Skid Row out, knowing it washes up at the doors and reaches for them, too. Skid Row comes for everyone, sooner or later.

An hour between buses, late night and morning mixed up, and Clifton's Cafeteria is around the corner. Just a few blocks south and west, across Harlem Place and Spring Street, and my dad says it's famous. Oh, it was a fine place in 1950, wasn't it though? Soda crackers in clam chowder, and the best coffee on the west coast. He checks his watch and decides we can do it if we hurry. Let's go, because we've lost our damn minds.

My dad walks beside me in the dark, oblivious to the L.A city that watches us cross her streets, smacking lips and checking the sharp edges on her teeth. This ain't 1950, fellas. You're lost.

Pathologically fearless my dad, nearly on the wild spectrum I think, looking back. I close my eyes and watch my memory of him. He isn't afraid of being eaten all up. His mind is gone wherever it goes, happy with his invisible music, and simply brooks no intrusion. He's seen the worst, and this isn't it. Not by a long shot.

Sometimes you just keep walking, and to hell with being scared.

It isn't a bad lesson to leave me with. I think about it sometimes when I'm afraid; him gray-haired, wearing his striped shirt and Gilligan hat and sneakers. The dealers, serial killers, demons, and tough guys all shuffle-step sideways, afraid to look him in the eye.

The coffee in Clifton's is just bad coffee, served on a plastic tray. The clam chowder is watery. The waiter doesn't care a bit, not at all, if anyone came here as a young man. 1950 was a long time ago, sir. My dad drinks his coffee and crumbles crackers anyway, vaguely angry that his ghosts have moved on and left him behind, never suspecting that he's a ghost too, now.

There are stories that the old Clifton's building on South Broadway is haunted, and that makes me smile. If dishes and napkins slide off tables, that's just us.

Me and my dad. Between buses, killing time.

Dear Ghost,

I dream sometimes about dead people, dreams so real that I wake up believing I summoned them. The phantoms know I miss them badly, and when I cry in my sleep, they hear me and come back. They make me coffee with cream and offer to cook bacon and eggs. We talk about the stupid things I've done, those hurtful things that weigh on me and make me sorry. They laugh at my foolishness, and after a minute I laugh, too.

Then I'm okay again.

My grade two teacher was Mrs. Triggs. She was young, blonde, pretty, and she had a brand-new husband, a brand-new teaching diploma, and a brand-new-for-1968 Chevelle. Yellow with a black vinyl roof, the Chevy had sharp lines and quad headlights and a fastback. It made quite a statement for an elementary school teacher in tiny Halstead, Kansas. Mrs. Triggs parked it where she could see it when she glanced up from her desk.

I loved cars, and it was probably the most perfect car I had ever seen. I was smitten. Some of that shine must have rubbed off on Mrs. Triggs because I thought she was perfect, too. I had a crush. I wanted her to like me.

The first day of school, she wrote something on the blackboard and pointed to me. I told her there was nothing at all on the blackboard, and I couldn't read what wasn't there. She told me to stand up, which was stupid because standing up doesn't change anything. I tried squinting, but the blackboard was still an empty expanse. Nothing there.

She marched me all the way to the very front, and it was my last chance.

The windows were open, because was still summertime. September was brand newborn and the sweet green blew in. I smelled bicycles and swimming and popsicles and wondered if anything could stop me if I climbed through the window and made a run for it.

I still couldn't see any writing and said so.

A girl named Laura sat in the front seat, wearing a pink dress. She was a good girl, the teacher's pet, and she laughed out loud. That gave the whole class permission to laugh. Mrs. Triggs smirked until she cottoned on that the laughter was at her, too. Her face turned red, and I was sent to the office.

My parents were called in for a meeting and she told them, officially, that I was stubborn or troubled or a smart ass, and probably all of those things. My mom had said so herself, many times, but she was young and pretty and didn't trust any teacher as young and pretty as she was. Teeth got bared.

Mrs. Triggs implied I would end up smoking and drinking and worse by the time I reached high school, if my parents didn't get a handle on my issues. Sitting here now, I look out my window at night snow and laugh, because she didn't know I would become a professional at those things and win championships.

My mom glared at me and said we would get an eye appointment, like she was damn sure I would have some explaining to do afterward. Of course, the eye doctor said I was blind as a bat, and my mom wanted to kill Mrs.

Triggs, but my dad said forget it, this whole thing is ridiculous. I wasn't in trouble after all, but I didn't win anything, because I got punished with thick glasses that became my ball-and-chain.

Every time the glasses got broken again playing hockey, every time I asked a girl to dance and she said no, I figured Mrs. Triggs got the last laugh.

I wanted to say I was sorry, that I hadn't wished for any of it. I only wanted her to like me, and for the rest of the year she didn't. I was only seven, and I already knew about school—this isn't going to be my thing. A lot of things weren't going to be my thing.

My dreams bring back the dead. They call, and in my reveries I let myself hear. My longings snap their leash, break free, and find the ones I miss.

The windows stay open in dreams. It's always summertime, September is brand newborn, and the sweet green blows in. I smell bicycles and swimming and popsicles. Nothing can stop me from climbing through the window, making a run for it…

…and finding you.

Dear Ghost,

In my mind's eye, 1982 is the last year before the colors got a little dim.

A Greyhound to L.A, and they still called it US Route 66 back then. Now it's mostly Interstate 40, endless miles of baking hardtop with all the romance and adventure of purgatory. Back then everybody, and I mean everybody—from Nat King Cole to the Rolling Stones—got their kicks on Route 66.

At twenty years old, a bus ticket, a backpack, and seventeen dollars seem like enough. The whole world is waiting. It's all possible, and it all smells fresh.

Dive south out of Chicago and leave winter and a broken heart behind. The Mississippi River in St. Louis is every Mark Twain thing it's supposed to be, and the world opens up into Joplin and Oklahoma City and all points west, all the way to Los Angeles and the shining sea. The big Greyhound bus jockeys with Steinbeck's migrant caravans and woody station wagons full of surf boards.

Forever is West, and we're all on the move.

Just past midnight in Amarillo, Texas, there's not much to see. The bus station is an island of dirty fluorescents in a colorless night. The air brakes hiss, and sleeping people stir in their seats. The bus is about half full, and nobody gets on or off. It's not a rest stop, just a pointless pause in the middle of no place. The front door has started to close when a figure crosses the platform and hits the steps at a dead run.

In those days, you could buy a ticket from the driver. They didn't like it much, as a rule. They had to consult mileage in a little book and make change, when you should have gone to the ticket window like everyone else. The conversation from the front sounds a little agitated, but eventually the transmission shudders into gear and the figure comes down the aisle, touching all the seat backs left-right-left, the way people do on a moving bus.

I sit halfway back, on the left side. I might be young, but I'm also a little bit old and this isn't my first rodeo. I know my way around the middle of the night in strange places. The front of the bus is where the busy people sit, people who want to sit beside you and eat baloney sandwiches and talk about themselves. The back of the bus is where the bad people go, and the street teaches that monsters are real. The middle is safe, the left side because it's ritual.

There's still enough passing light through the windows to resolve the figure into a young guy, about my age. He wears long hair and a jean jacket. He swings into the seat beside me, without asking if I mind. There are empty seats all over the bus, and my hackles raise. The lights of Amarillo are quickly gone, and the bus settles into a dark cruise.

"Look out the window on your side," the stranger blurts, with no introduction. He smells of sweat and cigarettes, even more than I do. "Tell me what you see."

He puts his seat and his head back, like he's hiding from the window. There's nothing outside now but pitch black. No house lights, no traffic, no reference points in the flat dark of Texas except dim stars. I tell him so, a little nervous.

"Keep watching. It should be soon. Don't look away."

A few miles pass and then the black vista opens up, all at once, into a strange tableau of flashing, spinning, blue-and-red light. The scene goes by so fast I have to check my own impressions after it's gone. A dark house, a dooryard opening off the highway, vehicles pulled in helter-skelter. The echoes of colored light pulse on the road shoulder for a few seconds, and then everything is black again.

"Cops," I say. "A little way off the road. Maybe an ambulance."

"How many cop cars?"

"I don't know," I tell him. "A lot. Four or five, at least."

He groans, a weird noise I haven't heard before. We had a sick dog once, and the stranger sounds like when the dog got close to the end. It scares me, a little.

"I might have killed someone," he says. "I guess I did."

"Maybe you should go up front and tell the driver," I suggest. "See if he'll let you get off here." It's an unbelievably stupid thing to say, but it's the best I can do. He ignores it, and starts to breathe funny. I know the sounds of a panic attack now, but in 1982 I didn't.

"I have someone waiting for me at the state line," he says. "How far is it?"

I'm not a fucking tour guide, I tell him. I'm not Mister Map. How am I supposed to know? I don't say any of it out loud, of course. In point of fact, I love maps and this route, and I know it well. I close my eyes so I can see the squiggle of 66 in my head.

"New Mexico line is about seventy miles," I say. "It's called Glenrio, but there's no town. It's just an abandoned gas station. The bus doesn't stop."

He leans forward and I feel his glare, even if I can't see it in the dark. "It can't be that far," he hisses. "That's over an hour away. They'll figure out I'm on this bus."

"Maybe it's less," I reassure him. Maybe it's more, I think. I'm just guessing.

I wait an interminable forty minutes and tell him I think we've gone far enough. He springs out of the seat and moves hand-over-hand to the front. Voices get raised, and the bus brakes hard onto the shoulder. The guy disappears into the night. I don't spot any headlights. I don't know if anyone waited for him. I'll never know what happened to him.

Hours later, the sun is coming up in Albuquerque. I catch the driver offloading bags onto the cement apron beside the bus. He's an adult, more than I am, and he's wearing a uniform. "The guy you let off at the state line told me he killed someone last night."

"What do you want me to do about that?" He stares at me. His eyes are flat. "People say all kinds of crazy things on the bus."

"I think he was telling the truth."

"The truth," he says, and sucks his cheeks. He straightens, hands on hips. "This bus leaves in fifteen minutes. If you're planning to call the cops, stay behind and do it after we pull out. Am I clear?"

He was clear, and I'm in my seat when the Greyhound wheels back onto the highway. The morning is getting warm, and the air conditioner comes on and puffs stale air. Hollywood is in front of us, and the blue Pacific is in front of us, and somewhere in front of us there's you. I don't know that finding you again is going to take another twenty-six years.

I'll hate myself for a long time for not being a hero. I'm going to loathe myself for sitting on that bus, beside a dragon, and doing nothing.

These days, the not-quite-old me would tell the young me that the stranger was another scared kid, and not likely to hurt anyone else. Maybe he did, though. Maybe he was a monster, just getting started. There are things we aren't meant to know.

Sometimes you can't be a hero. You protect the living and fix the things you can. Sometimes you just have to keep walking.

I know a couple of things.

Route 66 is what I'll take when my time here ends. We all head west, ghost. We all dead end at the beach. Passing through Joplin and Flagstaff might seem a little sad, since it's for the last time, but Route 66 runs out for everybody. It's just a highway after all, and not meant to go on forever.

There will always be dark nights and monsters, but everything perfect begins with an ending. I'll see you again. You'll be standing hipshot on Pacific sand, silhouetted against a warm red sun, waving.

I knew it, then. I know it, still.

Dear Ghost,

You told me once to count my dreams when I woke up, and to remember them so they'd be easier to shake off—or keep—depending on what I needed.

I close my eyes so I can count. Somewhere in the eighties, looking at a twilit Southern California street from the tiny balcony of a tiny apartment. This is another goodbye, but there's nobody to wave to. No hugs, no tears, just a couple garbage bags full of clothes, a few boxes of things I won't drag around much longer. Most of it is already downstairs, loaded into the car.

This small city carries the peculiar smell of watered desert, the odors of people, dogs, and garden hoses imposed on dry sand and chaparral. Everyone drives an MGB. They pretend to belong, but they all moved here last year and soon they'll be gone. They watch sitcoms, buy six-packs of light beer in green bottles, fire up barbeques in the evenings. They wear pastels and check every mirror to make sure their sunburns are holding up. They laugh a lot then look nervous because really, they don't know anyone or what they're supposed to do.

This time next year, they'll be back in Pennsylvania or Missouri, secretly relieved. Their ghosts will wander these dry streets, forever.

Below me, my car waits, squatted in the smell of gasoline and hot rubber. It's a Volkswagen Beetle at the moment, pale blue, built the year I turned twelve and you were still eleven. It's been a good one. Staunch and earnest, it starts and goes everywhere I ask it to. Nobody looks at it twice. Only a fool wants more than that.

There's a radio playing across the street. A young woman lives there with her small son. Donna Summer sings about bad girls—talking about sad girls. Toot-toot, beep-beep. I guess that's all the Saturday night you get when you have a little kid. Hot dogs and Kool-Aid for supper, a bath before bed. Television in the dark, one ear peeled. It sounds kind of nice. I think even if the young woman is lonely, she might be the only one here who is really home.

I'm tired, and Los Angeles is a couple hours south. The highway stays empty, old mountains tumbling into the ocean, until Sherman Oaks and the perfect signs that say Hollywood Blvd. and Sunset Blvd. and Western Ave. The Capitol Records building is forever, so my chest loosens a little the way it always does when I'm home.

I'm back tonight because I always come back and I always will. It's never late in L.A. It's home, and home has to take you back when you've run out of road.

Here's the thing though when the orange bleeds from the sky and it goes blue-dark:

I drive past unpretentious clubs that look like somebody's house, no big deal except for the valets peeling out in Aston Martins, past the liquor stores, bodegas, and arrows pointing to the beach. The traffic is a warm river of lights and music. Forget the smog because the air here is softer than anywhere in the world. The feel of Los Angeles air on your skin is life, death, and all the things between.

If you want to know what forever feels like, it's L.A wind. It's all you need.

Somewhere around Dodger Stadium, I stop at an intersection with no lights except the red one. No cars, no people, and all of a sudden midnight feels heavy. It's a scary place to see a baseball game. The little Volkswagen engine clatters patiently. I toss my cigarette out just in case I need to roll the window up.

There's a building on the nearest corner, tall for here. Old brick, it used to be something from back east, a factory or a warehouse. Back-east-things die here, so now it's just a broken-glass charcoal drawing. At the very top, a single window shows yellow light. I wonder who could live here, all alone in an empty building. I wonder if the rent is cheap when you get to the end of the world.

This city is paradise, but under the sun and sand and ten-dollar cocktails, Los Angeles is the loneliest place on earth. This is the land where all the clocks stop.

That's the deal—sun and shadow. You take it, or you fold your hand and go back east.

I close my eyes and wonder where you are and what you're doing tonight, ghost, here on this warm night in the middle part of the nineteen-eighties. Time is breathless. I think I'm starting to understand, and I wish so badly that I could be one of the lucky ones who count your change in a store, sit behind you in a movie theater, pass you on the sidewalk. I know this couldn't have happened any other way and it's a miracle it happened at all,

—but it's hard sometimes. It's hard, whenever I open my eyes.

Looking west at night, I've always seen lights across the ocean. Vast water, and maybe there's nothing out there closer than Japan and Samoa and Hawaii, but I see the lights anyway. I wonder if you look back at me, and you see lights too.

Remember, I have a blue Volkswagen, and it goes wherever I ask it to. I count my dreams now, and I remember them.

Dear Ghost,

It's Saturday night, time for hamburgers with ketchup, beans, and then my bath. My mom stands at the sink, listening to Rod McKuen on the record player, her hair tied up, clinking plates like she's running out of time. (She is.) My dad drinks bourbon and ginger ale with ice cubes, watching the last of the game. Hollywood nights are colored bright, but I only see little bits of them from my bedroom window.

Petula Clark sings "Downtown", while disembodied black-and-white feet walk across the stars in the television sidewalk, and that means toothpaste and it's my bedtime.

One day soon, I'll be my own boss and nobody will ever again tell me to go to bed. I don't know that, now. Tonight, I'll be tucked into the dark with my bear, sure this is forever.

It's Saturday night again, or maybe Sunday morning because I don't like wearing a watch. I sit on the hood of my car, headlights out, deep in the Toronto suburbs. All the houses look the same and all the people who live in them live tidy lives, doing the things they should. I don't belong here.

I love July, because even at midnight the air smells like barbeques and swimming pools. There's always a roller coaster somewhere, and it will always be summer. I have a fifth of lemon gin and a fresh pack of cigarettes under the front seat.

Around the corner and up a half block, a young woman is going to slide from her bedroom window and into the back yard. A minute later, she'll come running up the street, away from her sleeping parents, to me. I'll have the engine started by the time she reaches the car.

One day soon, she'll slide out another window—mine. She'll leave here for shiny buildings and a life with sparkling people. I don't know that, now. Tonight, I'm pretty sure she's going to be forever.

It's another Saturday night, and I'm sunk in the oldest part of the city. Cement and dirty brick, a short walk to a little corner store that's open late, because I haven't had dinner. The fellow behind the counter is strange and sad, and he puts my potato chips and chocolate milk into a small paper bag carefully, like he's packing me up to go on a trip. Maybe he is, but I don't know that yet.

Back to the dark sidewalk, and an old man approaches from the other direction. He's so zig-zag drunk he pats both hands on building walls like a map. When he gets close and the streetlights are right, I recognize my Latin teacher from tenth grade. His breathing is harsh, and he passes without seeing me. I'm too startled to say anything. I didn't know he lived around here. I never thought about him living anywhere.

Turning to watch him go, I worry his footsteps are where all roads lead. He drags a piece of me after him, but I don't know that, now. This dim city is forever, and it never lets you leave.

I don't know much, ghost, but I know this. You're the only one of us who never stopped eating snow when we switched to teevee dinners. When all our important grownups got old and died, when they tore down our houses to build glassy condominiums, when the girls and boys we thought we loved left us behind, we stopped believing in forever.

I know different now. Everything is forever, ghost. It's me who is passing through.

Someday, I'll open my front door and smell the early evening. I'll go outside and pause for a moment before I step into the warm drizzle. I'll settle my hat a little lower on my ears because catching a cold isn't a small thing at my age. I'll walk up to the corner and turn left. I'll stop to look around and feel happy when I recognize everything, but don't know where I am.

You'll be standing on the next corner, holding an umbrella over your head.

You look like the scene from a movie I can't quite remember, but I know I liked it. I can run again if I want to, but I don't. I want this to last, you waiting, all bright pastel in the blue and gray. When I'm close enough to hear you laugh, you'll close the umbrella. When it drops to the sidewalk at your feet, you'll grab my hands and turn your face up to the rain.

Everything is forever.

Dear Ghost,

Someone half the world away asked me just a little while ago if I believe in true love—if it really exists. Of course it does—and monsters, too. They go hand in hand. True love and monsters are the two things I'd bet my life on. I'd bet forever, in fact. I started to say so but hesitated...

...because you weren't there, to give me the right words.

When I was little, I found myself in the exact middle of one night at our kitchen door. I suppose I stood there in my cartoon-printed pajamas, wondering how I got there straight from sleep, but probably not. When you're little, you don't question the dancing of the Universe—especially at night.

There came movement in the darkness, a kind of sliding between cupboard and counter. A large tiger slinked into a faint pool of light from an outside bulb, like an actor coming on. She sat down on the linoleum in front of me.

"Hello," the tiger said, and licked her paw. "I'm going to eat you."

I froze. This cat had dark eyes, not yellow like the ones in picture books.

"All up," she said, in case I wasn't clear. "First, I'll break your heart."

The spell broke, so I turned to run, all the way to my mom and dad's room. They slept, humped shapes beneath their blankets. When I whimpered and shook them, they both sat up and reached out to touch me. Pale faces in the gloom, radiant warmth, the fragrances of sleep, and I got lifted into their bed. Sitting here decades later, a continent away, I realize that I could stop here and settle for the tiger and the smell of that bed, that room, those long-lost, lovely people. I don't need more proof of true love and monsters.

We aren't done with this story though, ghost. I shuddered, my breath hitched, I pointed into the dark hall.

"There's no such thing as tigers," my mom assured me, then probably blushed because that sounded silly. She liked to look good, even whispering in the dark. "In the kitchen, I mean," she amended. "None in the kitchen. You need a drink of water, that's all."

There are no tigers, they say, and they tell you the same thing about true love. There's sex, self-help books, and conditioned responses from well-adjusted people, but there's no such thing as true love. Even if there were, it wouldn't last forever. I suppose nobody wants to be responsible for the cracking of a million hearts if a few gold-and-black hairs ever got discovered on the kitchen counter.

"I'll chase it away," my dad said. "Tigers are not allowed in our house." He padded off, shirtless, striped-bottoms, and bare feet. I clutched my mom and wailed. I knew I would never see him again.

For a long time, I thought I never did. I believed the tiger came back to the room, looking like my dad and bringing me a glass of water. Monsters know a lot of spells, as a rule. Sometimes, when I turned into a teenager and my dad yelled at me about money or using the car or drinking too many beers, I remembered the tiger.

I think that's too simple though, ghost. I think there's a deeper truth, and it's true love.

I love a little girl with dark eyes, and a barefoot young woman wearing white lace. I love her first wrinkles squinting at lights on the ocean horizon, and an old woman who wonders if she could toss aside her cane and run across the sand. I love all your days, and I know where I was on every one of them.

I know who the tiger was, ghost, all those years ago. You did exactly what you promised. You broke my heart and showed me forever. Tigers keep their promises, so you ate me.

("All up," you whisper, smiling, and I nod.)

True love and monsters.

Dear Ghost,

They say no such thing as ghosts. I say it too, just to make you laugh.

Remembering impossible greenery and cold water from the hose—feeling so sad I can't breathe—times that are impossible to touch, ever again. Even the sunshine is so tinted it hurts. There's comfort in understanding that I don't need to understand.

There are no endings, and everything that matters is invisible, or nearly so.

I never imagined it wouldn't be dangerous. Things coalesce, hover above the path, and frighten. It's part of the deal, if the footprints get followed. You changed everything, and me, because you don't turn back when it gets dark and the rain starts.

If I don't see you for a while, that isn't the same as not loving you. I've been in love with you every day of your life, including this part of your life, when you've gone ethereal.

I watch the path. Love always.

I hope you feed the doves again.

Manufactured by Amazon.ca
Bolton, ON

27761842R00103